# Triumph in the Trenches

# Triumph in the Trenches

*The Green Book for Black Professionals*

Edited by Elona Washington
Publisher: The Author's Journey

# CONTRIBUTING AUTHORS

Dr. Natoshia Anderson, Ed.D.
Dr. Tauheedah Baker-Jones
Dr. Xenia Barnes, M.Ed.
James Bumpas, PMP, CSSBB, CSM, ITIL
Dr. Audrey C. Durrant
Judy Ellis
Dr. Mary Darden-Robinson
Dr. Carrie Young-McWilliams
Shareda M. Rollins
Ansar Saalih
Dr. Sherone Smith-Sanchez
Glynnis Swan
Dr. Wendy Talley
Nicole D. Vick
Phillip D. Woolfolk

ISBN: 979-8-9988072-7-5

Book Cover by Daniel O.

2nd edition 2025

# DEDICATION

This book is lovingly dedicated to every courageous reader and to all professionals who, like Dr. Claudine Gay and Dr. Antoinette "Bonnie" Candia-Bailey, have endured discrimination, hostility, and tragic loss in the fight for respect, equity, and inclusion.

# ACKNOWLEDGMENTS

We owe a heartfelt thank you to our Virtual Assistant, Olanma, affectionately called Ola. From the moment she joined this project, she brought a quiet, calm strength and steady professionalism that kept everything moving forward. Her eye for detail, her thoroughness, and her ability to stay composed in the midst of challenges gave this anthology the foundation it needed.

Ola showed up with care, consistency, and a spirit of excellence. Her presence reminded us that teamwork and dedication make the impossible possible. This book bears her imprint as much as anyone's, and we are deeply grateful for her.

*I have come to believe over and over again that what is most important to me must be spoken, made verbal and shared, even at the risk of having it bruised or misunderstood. That the speaking profits me, beyond any other effect. My silences had not protected me. Your silence will not protect you.*

—Audre Lorde, *Sister Outsider*

# CONTENTS

**CHAPTER 1**

P.O.L.I.S.H. .................................................................... 1

James Bumpas .........................................................

**CHAPTER 2**

THIS LITTLE LIGHT OF MINE............................. 12

Glynnis E. Swan .......................................................

**CHAPTER 3**

THE INVISIBLE TRENCH ................................... 24

Dr. Carrie Young-McWilliams...............................

**CHAPTER 4**

AUTHENTIC SELF-EXPRESSION AS AN ACT OF REVOLUTION

.................................................................................. 30

Dr. Xenia Barnes .......................................................

**CHAPTER 5**

A JEDI WARRIOR LEADS WITH GRACE............................ 41

Dr. Tauheedah Baker-Jones...................................

**CHAPTER 6**

FIGHTING CORPORATE STYLE ....................................... 58

Phillip Woolfolk .......................................................

**CHAPTER 7**

KETCH-A-FYAH!.......................................................... 69

Dr. Sherone Smith-Sanchez .................................

**CHAPTER 8**

A SEAT AT THE TABLE, NO VOICE IN THE ROOM ......................81

Dr. Mary Darden-Robinson... ................................................

**CHAPTER 9**

THE CALL IS COMING FROM INSIDE THE HOUSE ...................91

Nicole D. Vick ........................................................................

**CHAPTER 10**

EVEN WITH MY MOUTH CLOSED, I STILL SPEAK ................... 105

Dr. Natoshia Anderson............................................................

**CHAPTER 11**

ESCALATOR BLUES ...........................................................118

Shareda M. Rollins ..................................................................

**CHAPTER 12**

INTENT VS. IMPACT......................................................... 131

Wendy T. Talley ......................................................................

**CHAPTER 13**

THE CORPORATE MAZE.................................................... 145

Judy Ellis ...............................................................................

**CHAPTER 14**

INVISIBLE LEADERSHIP.................................................... 160

Ansar Saalih............................................................................

**CHAPTER 15**

EQUITY IN MEDICINE...................................................... 166

Audrey C. Durrant, MD............................................................

**JOURNAL**

REFLECTION QUESTIONS.................................................. 174

# FOREWORD

The thing about human nature that most of us refuse to accept is that it's undefeated. I don't mean that human beings haven't been conquered or subjugated in the course of human history. What I mean is that whenever people form groups, they tend to create a social hierarchy and consolidate power to rest in the hands of the few. Because human nature defaults to comfort then it's a reasonable expectation that those who are most privileged, powerful, and high status would be hard-pressed to relinquish those things willingly. In fact, in the history of human existence there has never been a group within a civilization who had the power to willingly give it up to a subordinate group. The only way that power has shifted from one group to another is by way of war or by cataclysmic event.

It's extremely important to acknowledge these truths as we examine the lived experiences of Black professionals in corporate contexts. We are navigating a construct that has evolved over centuries to become the modern expression of the colonial power structure. That being said, it's important to note that the model was never designed with humanity in mind. It was built to extract resources and labor from the subjugated for the benefit of the power dominant.

Additionally, the maxims of high productivity, high profitability at low-cost overhead are still the basic formula for business success. That means that exploitation is woven into the DNA of any corporate structure. When it comes to Black folks, who've only recently been afforded access to the prevailing lifestyles of our white counterparts, we must realize that the construct is nearly six hundred years old. We've only been recognized as full human citizens in the US for sixty years. That stark contrast is sobering, to say the least, but it should serve as a reminder that we're only at the front end of exploring what freedom feels like in this country as a people newly afforded access.

I coach many Black professionals on the underlying costs of the corporate climb. I begin by asking, "Why do you want to be in the c-suite?" and their answers typically fall into one of three categories. The first is usually related to ego. Meaning that they feel a sense of entitlement because of their education and a sense of pride in being the most knowledgeable and qualified to be in positions of higher authority based on their past performance in individual contributor roles or as middle managers. The second reason is the most obvious, which is that they want more money, and a higher title means a higher salary.

The third reason, however, is the most fascinating and the most telling. It falls under validation or filling a void. I find that so many of us are still wrestling with the marks of inadequacy and self-worth that 247 years of chattel slavery have left epigenetically imprinted upon our psyches. You see, excellence was not only required, but it was also engineered through trauma and wretched conditions, all for the benefit of the enslaver's enterprise. So today, we hold the belief that ascending to the c-suite will somehow provide us with a confirmation of value and respect that has eluded those before us. This thinking is not only foolhardy but also downright dangerous.

I see countless Black professionals sacrifice their physical and mental health trying to achieve a symbol of success that is reserved for only those who are willing to pay the price with their dignity, integrity, and cultural identity. All to enter the rooms that have been reserved for the power dominant as if to say that arrival will somehow wash away the stains of their ancestry in the eyes of the gatekeepers.

The truth is that since Fortune began compiling its list of 500 top-performing companies in 1966, there have been nearly 2000 CEOs at the helms of these organizations. Out of those 2000, only 25 have been Black. This is by no means an accident. I've had the opportunity to speak to one of the 25 Black CEOs who was the head of one of the largest pharmaceutical companies in the world.

When I asked him what his cost for the climb was, he immediately answered, "Time with family and milestone moments with the kids." But upon deeper reflection for a moment, he looked at me and said that he still to this day regrets the amount of cultural identity suppression he endured to get into the rooms reserved for the power dominant. That chilling realization begs the question, is the climb worth the cost?

I encourage the reader to examine their own motivations for seeking to elevate in corporate spaces. In this introspective effort, I challenge you to ask yourself a few questions. For starters, I want you to answer, if you can, if your desire to rise to the top is an inherent desire or if it is a reflection of a prior generational program that you're executing in full automaticity.

The battery in most of our backs was placed there by our foreparents who desperately sought access. They'd say, Go to school, get a good education, get a good job, work 30 years, retire, and die." This was the script most of us read as we were ushered into the fray. The challenge is that our fore parents had no idea what was on the other side of access. All they knew is that they were denied entry, and if their children are now able to experience it, then by all means they will.

It is said that the thing you're denied most becomes the object of your desire. What they were denied most was access to a white lifestyle. Today, we're born into access and find ourselves the freest Negroes this country has ever seen, but we have an opportunity to question whether access is worth the cost that comes with it. If admission means giving up your community, your culture, your language, your identity, and even your health, then I think the question answers itself.

As you progress through the following pages, you will hear from Black professionals who have worked the corporate plantation and lived to tell the stories. In an exposé of what it's like to be second guessed, demeaned, over talked, underappreciated, overlooked, under-valued, and overworked, you may find some of their stories hard to stomach.

But the beauty lies in the imperfections of these harsh truths. Let their truths be a beacon of light that shines upon the hideous underbelly of the corporate construct. May their unanswered pleas to human resources, now be met with open ears and open hearts of you, the reader.

If you are someone who sits in a position of power and are reading these experiences in horror, allow yourself to steep in the fullness of this moment of humanity. The payoff is one of expansion that only exposure to experiences that differ from yours can bring. Do not turn away; do not shield your eyes. Absorb, process, reflect, then do something with your newfound knowledge.

May you be forever changed by what you read, and may that change translate into tangible relief for those who have paid the exceedingly high cost for their climb.

In Light,

John Graham, Author
*Plantation Theory: The Black Professional's Struggle Between Freedom & Security*
www.plantationtheory.com

# PREFACE

For years, I did everything right. I earned the degrees, joined the committees, sought out mentors, and made myself visible to leadership. I watched as my ideas were adopted—often by others who presented them as their own. I noticed the shift in the room when I solved problems or offered solutions. And like so many Black professionals, I internalized it all. I convinced myself that I was the problem, that I needed to work harder, be smarter, stay quieter, or somehow become more... palatable.

Then I heard the term, "you bring your whole self to work," and everything made sense.

Our parents marched and boycotted for desegregated schools, workplace equality, and an end to employment discrimination, believing we would be given the same fair treatment and opportunity as our white counterparts. But what we actually inherited were workplaces where white people also brought their whole selves to work, their biases, prejudices, and racism. And colleagues of all backgrounds brought their insecurities and blind spots—the resentment, the competition, the need to prove they earned their seat. And among ourselves, we brought lateral gatekeeping, respectability politics, and the fear of being "too Black" or not Black enough. So we stepped into institutions designed with systemic barriers to block our success and compromise our mental wellness. Some of us figured out how to navigate these systems. Most of us are still trying.

But what if the problem was never about cracking a code? What if the real power lies in seeing the system clearly and choosing whether to navigate it, disrupt it, or leave it behind? THAT is the purpose behind this anthology.

You can find books by Black authors that detail these experiences and offer frameworks for healing and thriving. I could have written one myself, as could any of the co-authors in this series. Instead, I chose to compile their stories to prove a critical point: It doesn't matter if you're an executive or entry-level. It doesn't matter if you have a PhD or a high school diploma. It doesn't matter if you're in tech, healthcare, finance, or education. These patterns show up everywhere, for all of us.

That's why this anthology features Black men and women from all walks of life—different management levels, different degrees, different industries, different paths. When you see yourself in a story from someone with a similar background, it's affirmation that you're not crazy. When you see yourself reflected in a story from someone with a completely different background, the message becomes undeniable: You are not the problem. The system was designed for you to fail.

Our stories, taken alone, can be dismissed. But together, they are too loud to ignore. As the African proverb says, if you want to go fast, go alone. If you want to go far, go together. We've gone far enough to see the system clearly. Now it's time to come together and decide what comes next.

In triumph,

Elona Washington, Chief Publishing Officer
The Author's Journey

# INTRODUCTION

## Why The Triumph Series Exists

The Triumph in the Trenches series was born out of urgency and a refusal to stay silent.

For too long, Black professionals have been told that workplace challenges are individual problems requiring individual solutions. Work harder. Be more resilient. Adjust your tone. Prove your worth—again. But the truth is, what we face isn't personal failure. It's systemic design. And that design is costing us our mental health, our dignity, and sometimes our lives.

This series exists because we need more than survival strategies. We need recognition, resolve, rebuilding, and REST.

## Why It Matters Now

The workplace has become a battleground—not just for promotions or recognition, but for our mental health, our dignity, and our survival. What happens in corporate offices, hospitals, schools, and courtrooms follows us home. It shows up in our communities as we watch talented, brilliant people break under the weight of systems designed to exploit and exclude us. It shows up in our bodies as chronic stress, anxiety, and burnout— what public health researchers call "weathering," the accelerated physical deterioration caused by cumulative exposure to social and economic disadvantages. Studies show that by age 49-55, Black women have the biological markers of white women who are 7.5 years older.

And the system isn't just unfair, it's calculating. In 2025, over 300,000 Black women and 200,000 Black men lost their jobs.

Not because of merit.
Not because of performance.

But because the institutions we gave our labor, our brilliance, and our loyalty to were systematically pushing us out.

This series exists because silence and survival aren't enough anymore.

**How the Volumes Connect**
Each volume serves a distinct purpose, forming a complete journey:
Volume 1: Recognition — Identify the patterns clearly and understand that the system, not you, is broken. You cannot resolve or rebuild what you refuse to see. This volume validates your experience and gives you the language to name what's been done to you.
Volume 2: Resolve — Navigate the system with strategic determination. Contributors show you how to fight when it's worth fighting, endure when you must, and protect your peace while doing both.
Volume 3: Rebuilding — Heal and rebuild beyond the system. This volume offers pathways to reclaim your power, restore your mental health, and build a life on your own terms, whether inside the workplace or beyond it.

And woven throughout all three is REST—not as passivity, but as strategic pause. REST means stopping to think instead of reacting. It means being intentional about your next move. It means protecting your mental and emotional energy so you can move with clarity and power.

**What's Inside**
Across all three volumes, each includes:
Personal essays from Black professionals across industries, management levels, and backgrounds who share what they've endured and overcome
Frameworks and strategies you can implement immediately, from documenting discrimination to setting boundaries to building support systems
Reflection questions at the end of the book to help you process and apply what you've learned

Direct access to contributors so you can connect with them for coaching, consulting, or continued conversation
An invitation to the Triumph community where we support each other beyond these pages

You won't just read about workplace trauma; you'll gain tools to navigate it, challenge it, heal from it, and move beyond it.

**This Is for You**
Whether you're in the trenches right now, navigating with strategic resolve, or healing and rebuilding beyond the system, this series is for you.

If you've ever been told you're too sensitive, too aggressive, or "not a culture fit," this is for you.

If you've watched your ideas get stolen, your competence questioned, or your presence treated as a problem, this is for you.

If you're exhausted from performing excellence in spaces that refuse to see or reward you, this is for you.

And if you're ready to stop surviving and start thriving, whether inside the system or beyond it, this is definitely for you.

**A Note on the Series Structure**
This introduction appears only in Volume 1 to establish the vision and arc of the entire Triumph in the Trenches series.

Volumes 2 and 3 will not include additional introductions; they move straight into the stories.

The series concludes with an afterword in Volume 3 that reflects on the complete journey, what we've learned together, and how we move forward both individually and collectively.

Let's begin.

# JOIN TRIUMPH

A free community for readers serious about personal and professional growth.

To join, use the QR code feature on your phone and scan the above code.

Or type skool.com/triumph-7369 in your browser.

# 1

# P.O.L.I.S.H.
## A Light Gon' Shine

### JAMES BUMPAS

*No one lights a lamp and then puts it under a basket. Instead, a lamp*
*is placed on a stand, where it gives light to everyone in the house.*
—Matthew 5:15, NLT

Let me frame up my chapter—this entire book—properly for you. You see, this anthology of overcoming and being triumphant even when we are treated like we could never rise from the trenches is all about equipping you with the keys to unlocking the doors to corporate success. That is, we are tasked with imparting wisdom and sharing insights so you can thrive and, in turn, help others.

With over three decades of coaching, mentorship, and leadership, I hope to share a unique perspective of being a Black man. I do not offer my viewpoint to challenge or overshadow any of the amazing authors in this book, most of whom are powerfully talented and visionary Black women. I have found that being a Black man represents a significant threat to some white people.

Let me rephrase that: being a "competent, confident, and educated Black man" represents a significant threat.

As I close this introduction, it is important to note that this chapter is not about the difficulties we face in the workplace or who causes them; it's about how we overcome those difficulties. I mean, who are we on the other side of the difficulties? Did we cut corners to get around them? Did we give up, throw in the proverbial towel, and let the white people dictate who we are? Did we betray our own belief system or core values to get revenge, hurting ourselves or other people along the way? Or did we handle things in such a way that we are now better people for it? P.O.L.I.S.H.

I have been blessed to serve in several different capacities for many global high-tech companies. In my experience as a leader and hiring manager, I cringed when young or inexperienced Black or brown candidates failed to demonstrate key interpersonal skills that ultimately led to us selecting another candidate. That happened a lot. I was constantly torn between a desire to give my people a chance at a great-paying job and the need to choose the best, most capable and skilled candidate for the job. However, without the skills I deemed necessary, I knew I could not, in good conscience, do what some of my white counterparts have done for generations and choose based on ethnicity.

Sensing that this was a systemic issue, I called upon friends from the Black community, several of whom served in HBCUs and various companies, to form a Black Leadership Think Tank. I asked them if my experience was an outlier due to the highly technical nature of my industry or if it was more commonplace. While they agreed that it was indeed a real problem, they could not or would not contribute to a meaningful solution. So, I set out to design and develop a relatively low-cost and readily available solution to empower our people to flourish not only in corporate America but also in the broader global workplace. The following are the six major skill gaps I noticed:

1. How a person communicates.
2. How open a person is to receiving advice or wisdom

from others.

3. The person's view on leadership.
4. The person's view (thoughts) of themselves.
5. The person's knowledge of and ability to articulate their strengths.
6. The person's level of connectedness or willingness to help others or serve a cause greater than their own.

Taking this into account, I created the P.O.L.I.S.H. Mentorship Program:

**P** - Public Speaking
**O** - Objective Mentoring
**L** - Leadership Skills
**I** - Image/Branding
**S** – StrengthsFinder
**H** – Helping Others/Community Service

In this chapter, I demonstrate how these six skills helped a group of inexperienced summer interns succeed, assisted my information technology department in achieving its goals, and helped our external customers achieve theirs.

## YOU CANNOT HELP IT

*It's always darkest before the dawn...*

—Thomas Fuller

I discovered that I had an affinity for coaching and mentoring in the United States Navy. When new aviation electricians joined the department, it became apparent that the few assigned to me excelled because I took a vested interest in their success and built meaningful relationships with them. The number of my team members grew and changed as sailors transitioned to different ships and military commands around the world. However, I never forgot how great it felt to sow good seeds and watch them reap through the lives of others as they served.

Fast-forward to the business world, and I look back fondly, recalling that I, too, had great leaders who sowed into my life through mentoring. Reluctant to play the proverbial race card, I could no longer deny that systematic racism runs rampant in corporate America. Whether it's nonprofit, public health, military, etc. every organization lowers the bar when it comes to combating racism. Yes, you heard that right. As you will undoubtedly notice as you read the amazing accounts from my fellow triumphant Black authors, the higher you climb the corporate ladder, the more severe the attacks. But the attacks will also come very early in your career too...

\*\*\*

Coffee, car keys, and cell phone in hand? Check! Laptop? Check! Man, I am super excited to get to work! Our Account Executive (AE) has approved my summer internship program. P.O.L.I.S.H. is being piloted, and today's the first day our department will begin training three rising local college seniors to participate. And yes. They will be paid.

I make it to the office and introduce myself. After they give their introductions, I see how afraid all three of them are. None of them has had the opportunity to work in a large company's information technology department. They are completely star-struck. So, I take them into a conference room to complete paperwork and to get to know them better. I want to set them at ease by going over expectations for the summer and how, together, we will partner for success.

My first requirement, I tell them, is to have fun. I pause for effect. Then I see them visibly relax. Since it is quite relevant to this story, I must share that demographically, one student is a young Black man from an HBCU, another is a young Latina from a private university, and the third is a young white man from a state university.

I later assigned the interns to their project managers; they would be supporting them in working on important initiatives for the business. Another benefit of working with the project managers was that it facilitated meaningful and real-world work experience for the students. In addition to the internship, mentoring was also a large component of the summer program. So, I met with the students each week to allow them to brief me on four things:

1. What did you do?
2. What did you learn?
3. What went wrong?
4. What would you like to learn next?

I used these questions to teach the interns about the first three letters of P.O.L.I.S.H. For 'P', public speaking, the interns prepared PowerPoint presentations and presented their content to me. For 'O', objective mentoring, I asked the students to drive their own performance review discussions by proactively answering these questions each week. Finally, the 'L' for leadership, while broad in application, was demonstrated in two ways. First, I wanted them to discuss my leadership of the mentorship program. Secondly, I assessed how the interns were leading themselves as they met the expectations I set.

Each week, the students succeeded in reporting against the performance expectations. In parallel, I requested candid feedback from the project managers working with the interns. I held one-on-one meetings with the interns to share the feedback from their respective project managers so they could improve as necessary.

As we proceeded through the program, I pitched an end-of-summer project idea to the AE. I requested some of his time for the three students to present what they accomplished during the program and to demonstrate the value they brought to the department and the customers served. The AE considered the idea. He said, almost to himself, "Well, two-thirds would not be a bad return on our investment." I was taken aback. I said, "Excuse me; did you say something?" My initial thought was that if I acknowledged that I had heard him speak, he might choose not to repeat it. However, he shocked me and continued, "I heard from one of the project managers that the intern that went to one of those party schools, those HBCUs, did not impress him."

I expressed my shock while remaining as composed as I could while stating that I had documentation to suggest otherwise. My documentation showed all three interns had performed well all summer. Hence, I wanted them to present their results to our department executive as a celebration and reward. The AE said, "He went to an HBCU; I mean, we must include them in our Summer Intern Mentorship Program, but I do not expect you to be able to get real work performance out of him. You cannot help it..." Surprisingly, unperturbed by my rising anger, the AE eventually relented and allowed me to prepare the interns for the final presentation.

I had some work to do to make sure that the young Black man had a fighting chance amongst his peers. You see, in a lot of ways, this young man represented so many Black men, Black people holistically in corporate America.

Coming from the inner city, this young man had already overcome the amazing odds of a single-parent home, gangs, and a failed public education system that pushed him through relatively ill-prepared to be a contributing member of society. But his mother and other loving members of his family and community encircled him and helped him find his way. He was a very intelligent young man, and he was now one school year away from being a first-generation college graduate and the pride of his family. However, his manner of speaking in the office, like he was talking in the streets back home, did not convey how brilliant his mind was. He was raw and unrefined, like a diamond hidden within a lump of coal.

## BRING YOUR BEST
*To shine your brightest light is to be who you truly are.*
—Roy T. Bennett

Working with all three interns and still performing my

duties as a senior IT project manager and an organizational effectiveness lead, I still knew I needed to do more to equip the young brother with the tools to succeed, not only in this final presentation but also in corporate America. So, together, we spent an additional two hours each week after work and one hour on Saturday mornings over breakfast. I taught, and he listened. He spoke, and I critiqued. We laughed and bonded during these extended one-on-one sessions. I explained the power of our brand and our image, the 'I' in P.O.L.I.S.H. Finally, one Saturday morning after breakfast, he asked the question that I knew was going to come... "Why are you spending more time with me than you are with the other two interns? Am I really that slow?"

"Slow? Absolutely not!" I told him that, through no fault of his own, he had a longer path to take to reach the same destination as the other two interns. I shared that he is just as intelligent and hardworking as they are, but he was being judged because of the skin he was in and by the HBCU he was attending. I did not sugarcoat the realities that I face every day as a Black man in corporate America. My performance, while stellar when compared to the 'leaders in title only' in my peer group, still rendered me invisible as a leader in the eyes of the white people in power. (Fellow author Ansar Saalih will speak to Invisible Leadership in his chapter.) I told him that he too would face many of the same struggles because he was an educated, competent, and confident Black man.

## A LIGHT GON' SHINE

*Nothing can dim the light which shines from within.*

—Maya Angelou

And so, we worked... Hard! When we discovered word pronunciations that presented too much difficulty, we selected other synonyms. As he continued, his confidence grew. He practiced his script with the other interns and willingly received feedback from them. He even offered suggestions that helped them improve their slide decks. I provided each of them with copies of the *Strengthsfinder 2.0* book by Gallup and Tom Rath, which contained the code to complete the CliftonStrengths® assessment. This assessment reveals an individual's strengths, or the 'S' in P.O.L.I.S.H. This assessment is a gift to the interns to unpack the power of understanding your own strengths, what happens when you overuse a strength (weakness), and the interactions of your strengths when you collaborate or clash with others.

The interns had all worked so hard to prepare a great presentation, and I was very proud of them. On the inside, I must admit that I was positively ecstatic at the growth and perseverance of my young brother through the span of one summer. At this point in time, I no longer cared about the opinion of the AE because I knew without a doubt that the interns not only delivered tangible benefit to the company and value to our customers, but they also learned some valuable skills that, when utilized, helped them succeed in corporate America. This was especially true for the young Black man.

## How Did They Do?

Come on, you know I couldn't leave you hanging like that! They provided copies of their monthly performance reviews and a paper copy of their presentation to the AE. At the appropriate time, each of them stood up, walked to the front of the conference room, and gave their presentations utilizing Microsoft PowerPoint. They delivered it to an audience of business executives, their assigned project managers, and other IT team members from our department. The interns took their time explaining to the AE what they did all summer, what they learned, and the differences they made. They were calm under pressure, and they smiled not only because I was exceptionally proud of them but also because they were also quite proud of themselves! They delivered their presentations flawlessly!

## WHERE ARE THEY NOW?

*Do not repay evil with evil. Do not retaliate with insults when people insult you. Instead, pay them back with a blessing. That is what God has called you to do, and he will grant you his blessing.*

—1 Peter 3:9 NLT

Upon seeing how pleased the business executives were over the success of the first summer intern mentorship program, the AE greeted the interns and gave them a short speech of appreciation. He spoke as if the program was all his idea from the beginning. Then he extended a hand to me, congratulating me on a job well done for mentoring the team and leading the program to a successful end. As I shook his hand, I kept my anger and my attitude at bay. He said something insignificant, probably an attempt to gaslight me. I cannot recall; it was truly that unimportant. Six months later, I tendered my letter of resignation from that company.

The young Latina who attended an elite private university has stayed in touch with me, and I am always glad when I hear from her. She readily admits that since then, she has faced her own struggles as a Latina woman. She decided that working in IT was not for her. She is quite successful in business finance.

The young white man who attended the state university graduated and worked in IT for several years. We went to lunch many times to catch up, and he amazed me with how humble and down-to-earth he has stayed over the years since our summer program together. While moving up the corporate ladder, he requested a couple references and still refers to me as his mentor.

Lastly, the young Black man moved back home after graduating college—which he achieved with honors! He chose not to work in IT. Instead, he opted for more philanthropic work in his community and through his local church. He sings and is involved in music production. He told me that he is still trying to find his calling. I told him, "Aren't we all, my friend? Aren't we all?"

## An Honorable Mention

It would be remiss of me not to mention that on one of those Saturdays after breakfast, I took the three interns with me to support an Adopt-A-Highway community clean-up event. This event is an example of the last letter in P.O.L.I.S.H. The 'H' for 'Helping Others'. Community outreach, or service, allows us to temporarily divert our attention away from our own situations. In doing this, we not only realize that we typically have it better than we thought we did, but we also inspire hope in others. In addition, it is great for the heart!

So, I promised them a good lunch afterwards as an incentive to keep them motivated, recalling that I had to do such things like that with my own children. However, they never complained; they never fussed or half-assed the entire three hours of collecting trash up and down the side of the highway. That really made me proud. I was so proud, in fact, that I asked them over lunch why they didn't complain. The young lady spoke first. She said, "Do you think that was hard or worth complaining about, Mr. Bumpas? That was just a way to give back... That was nothing." The other two interns just smiled and nodded their heads in agreement as they hastily ate their double cheese and pepperoni pizza. Their generation sometimes gets a bad rap, but they give me hope for the future...

***

When I first created the P.O.L.I.S.H. solution, I called it "POLISHED". I would like to share that the 'ED' stands for education, as in continuous education. Reading at a very young age opened my eyes and exposed my mind to concepts, ideas, and people that I otherwise would not have had access to growing up in the racist South. I encourage you to read often and to employ others to do the same. Never stop learning.

As a Black person, you will undoubtedly face adversity, racism, classism, sexism, and cronyism in corporate America. You will need to "POLISH" your armor to keep it shining. You will need to keep on shining to keep inspiring others. You will need to inspire others to make a difference. Just like they're counting on me, I am counting on you. Shine On!

---

James Bumpas
www.btstriumphwithjames.com/polish
James Bumpas, PMP, CSSBB, CSM, ITIL leverages his 30+ years as an IT expert and founder of a tech consulting firm, providing mentoring and coaching rooted in emotional intelligence to improve business processes and guide software programs.

# 2

# THIS LITTLE LIGHT OF MINE
## Outshining Stereotypes & Biases

GLYNNIS E. SWAN

"Welcome to [dream job]. First, I want to let you know that you are a diversity hire, and the company has invested a lot in ensuring you're happy here...".

"Um...thank you...uh." Wait, what? *Diversity hire?* What the heck? Is my boss saying this to me on my *first day of work*? Stop. Don't overreact. Maybe I'm misunderstanding. Just nod and smile.

"And I know you have an impressive resume, but you're on a high-performing team now, and you need to prove to them that you belong here."

Despite my best efforts to maintain a cheerful expression, I forcefully swallow the information that I have just been told I am a diversity hire. How do I respond? Do I thank *them* for the opportunity for which *I* worked so hard? I earned this, didn't I? I have to say something, but I'm about to make the most money in my career, and I don't want to mess that up. I try to speak, but the words are jumbled, caught in a massive lump in my throat. I'm sweating. I want to throw up. My hands are shaking, so I sit on them. Suddenly, my shoulders ache, and I see black flashes, then red. It's hard to breathe. It's been 7 seconds since I've experienced all these feelings. Panic and confusion quickly give way to anger. How dare you minimize my achievements? I must prove myself! That's what I want to say. But instead, I continue to smile and nod through the rest of the conversation, barely hearing anything else. Why do I feel like I've had my voice physically beaten out of me by someone on a video call hundreds of miles away? When asked at the end of my *welcome*, "Any questions or concerns?" I finally managed to speak. "Nope, I'm so happy to be here and look forward to working with the team!" Really? I don't feel welcomed at all. I silently sucked my teeth... broken on the first day.

Every day I entered the corporate battlefield, I donned an invisible cloak of armor, priding myself on my resilience and letting xenophobic comments roll off my back because I'm usually the first *me* they've ever met. But really, that feeling in my chest isn't pride; it's the slow, painful erosion of my dignity. I leave work exhausted from the mental gymnastics of appeasing clients, vendors, managers, and colleagues who encourage me to be my authentic self while denigrating my accent, hair, complexion, education, and even *perceived* socio-economic status.

In 25 years, I've experienced more than my share of unwelcoming corporate American spaces, having been stereotyped, scapegoated, and discriminated against during every phase of employment. I've always strived for excellence and have had notable accomplishments, yet I often doubt my capabilities or wonder if I deserve to be valued and respected. Unfortunately, I am not alone. Every day, underrepresented professionals experience microaggressions, are "othered," and are made to feel as if they don't belong. And we're told that "if this is constantly happening to you, it must be you." No, it is not you.

Between July 2020 and December 2023, I coached and mentored 503 adult persons of color across various industries in the United States, the United Kingdom, Mexico, Bermuda, and the Caribbean to map their careers, navigate corporate environments, manage conflict, and become influential leaders. Of the 464 individuals identifying as females with at least three years of corporate work experience, an overwhelming 91% cited incidents of stereotyping and bias, including discrimination, gaslighting, harassment, and bullying in the workplace. An even more dismal statistic is that 100% of my clients delayed seeking help due to self-blame.

This trend is having disastrous long-term effects on people of color. We tout resiliency like a badge of honor, not recognizing that it's neither normal nor healthy to be continuously gaslit. We have been fooled into thinking that covering is coping. We don't understand what's happening while it's happening and feel stupid when we finally figure it out *after* we've been terminated or blackballed. We are experiencing the same mental effects as people who have been physically or emotionally abused, and we're told it's not real *trauma*. Workplace trauma is real. Let's shift our mindset to acknowledge our unique corporate challenges and embrace empowering strategies to help overcome them.

## STEREOTYPING, BIAS, AND INTERSECTIONALITY

*Stereotyping* can be defined as assigning generalized characteristics or traits to a particular group based on preconceived notions or assumptions,[1] and *bias* is the tendency to favor or disfavor individuals or groups due to those pre-existing beliefs.[2] As a Black female, disabled, U.S. immigrant from a small British territory, intersectionality is a crucial aspect of my identity. Intersectionality recognizes that individuals can face multiple forms of discrimination (or privilege) *simultaneously*, acknowledging the complex interplay of not only race and gender but several other social identities.

While I've certainly experienced stereotyping, bias, and overt discrimination throughout my career, it's the

---

[1] Worthy, L D. 2020. "Stereotypes, Prejudice and Discrimination." Pressbooks. July 27, 2020.
https://open.maricopa.edu/culturepsychology/chapter/stereotypes-prejudice-and-discrimination/.
[2] "Dictionary.com | Meanings & Definitions of English Words." 2021. In Dictionary.Com. https://www.dictionary.com/browse/bias.

microaggressions—those subtle, often unintentional, discriminatory comments or behaviors—that continue to threaten my identity. I typically encounter microaggressions that stem from assumptions about my identity, education, socioeconomic status, ethnicity, culture, or abilities, reinforcing the intersectional challenges I am forced to navigate. I may face the expectation of conforming to stereotypical notions of femininity while simultaneously grappling with racial biases that may undermine my professional or personal capabilities.

In 2021, I was one of three panelists speaking at a session on corporate diversity at a global conference. While attending the same meeting the following year, I ran into one of the panelists who didn't recognize me because "you're wearing flats, and your hair is different" (silk press vs. braids). This person introduced themselves as if we'd never met before, even though they had commended me for being "so articulate" the previous year. I didn't understand; I worked for a top company and was one of the few leaders of color to present at the event on corporate diversity, nonetheless. Yet, at that moment, I was insignificant, a nobody. I silently pondered: Was I just a Black face to fill a quota on the diversity panel? Did anything I presented even matter? Do I belong here, and more importantly, *how can I fix this*? Sadly, to fix others' perceptions of us, we often "cover."

## COVERING

Stereotypes, bias, and subsequent discrimination can have lasting effects on both individuals and the corporate culture, two of the most damaging being "covering" and "imposter syndrome."[1] A recent study conducted by Deloitte and the Melzer Center for Diversity, Inclusion, and Belonging at The NYU School of Law investigated the magnitude of behaviors in which 1,269 US

---

[1]"New Deloitte Study Reveals Most US Workers 'Cover' Their Identities at Work to Their—and Their Employers'— Detriment." Deloitte. November 14, 2023. https://www2.deloitte.com/us/en/pages/about-deloitte/articles/press-releases/deloitte-deiinstitute-uncoveringculture.html.

employees "cover" or "downplay known disfavored identities to fit into mainstream corporate cultures." The research explores perceptions of authenticity, power, and psychological safety while navigating workforce equity and belonging. NYU's Chief Justice Earl Warren Professor Kenji Yoshino defined the axes of behaviors on which individuals cover:[1]

- Appearance-based: how individuals alter their self-presentation, including grooming, attire, and mannerisms, to blend into mainstream culture.
- Affiliation-based: how individuals minimize behaviors widely associated with their identity, often to negate common stereotypes.
- Advocacy-based: not defending or promoting the interests of one's group.
- Association-based: how individuals avoid contact with other group members.

The survey respondents' social identities included:
1. Age
2. Caregiver status
3. Disability (Dependent Adult or Child)
4. Education
5. Gender
6. Immigration status
7. Mental health status
8. Military status
9. Race/Ethnicity
10. Religious affiliation
11. Sexual orientation and gender identity
12. Socioeconomic status (current/childhood)

---

[1] Yoshino, Kenji. 2006. *Covering: The Hidden Assault on Our Civil Rights*. New York: Random House Inc.

While the practice of covering spans across all workplace demographics, the study revealed that it is most prevalent among individuals with multiple marginalized identities. 71% of employees with five or more marginalized identities reported covering at work, compared to 56% with 1 or 2 marginalized identities. Other astonishing statistics[1] show:

- 80% of Black women reported covering at work, compared to 43% of Black men.
- 93% of Black employees with disabilities reported covering, compared to 60% of white employees.
- 100% of Black LGBTQ+ employees reported covering.

Various reasons were cited for covering, such as avoiding negative stereotypes or judgments, organizational advancement, or keeping their job. Over 50% of all employees reported an increased need to cover based on their interactions with managers and above. Though I feel confident in my identity, this prompted me to think about how and why I've covered throughout my career. I've certainly done so for all the reasons mentioned above, usually covering to appease the convenience or comfort of others. In the past, I have:

- Toned down my native accent.
- Chosen "professional" hairstyles.
- Accepted the mispronunciation of my name.
- Hidden the fact that I was a 19-year-old unwed mother.
- Downplayed struggles or did not seek accommodation due to disability.

## Imposter Syndrome

I am in the company of 75% of U.S. female corporate leaders who have experienced imposter syndrome throughout their careers.[1] Yuck, imposter syndrome, a name that unjustly blames its victims as opposed to the "systemic racism, classism, xenophobia, and other biases"[2] that create this wretched phenomenon. An archaic notion focused on "fixing women at work instead of fixing the places where women work."[4]

I knew there was nothing I did not deserve or could not accomplish thanks to a fearless Black mother, aunts, and grandmothers. Thus, I struggled to understand when, during my life, I developed this debilitating mindset. It wasn't until I started writing this chapter that I recalled something that years of therapy could not unearth: the first time I questioned my competence.

First year of high school. Parent-Teacher Conference Night. I was 12. My elementary school test scores presented an opportunity to attend Bermuda's prestigious Warwick Academy High School. Founded in 1662, it's reputed to be the oldest school in continuous operation in the Western Hemisphere. I was eager to be immersed in a new learning culture, and I just knew my mom would come home with glowing reports from all my teachers. But, of all the reports my mom shared that night, I only remember hearing, "You *must* prove this woman wrong." Mrs. H, my first-year English teacher, was a blonde-haired, blue-eyed, self-described "ideal candidate for Hitler's master race" (as told during her depiction of being a young British girl in the early 1940s while we were studying The Diary of Anne Frank). Mrs. H told my mother that "although she seems bright and may have been at the top of her class *where she comes from*," I shouldn't expect to do as well at this school. Excuse me?

I was an excellent student. I worked hard, earned my spot, and never considered myself less deserving than others. Until that night. I allowed someone to dim the light in my soul, setting a

---

[1] "KPMG Study Finds 75% of Female Executives across Industries Have Experienced Imposter Syndrome in Their Careers." KPMG. October 7, 2021. https://info.kpmg.us/news-perspectives/people-culture/kpmg-study-finds-most-female-executives-experience-imposter-syndrome.html.
[2] Tulshyan, Ruchika, and Jodi-Ann Burey. "Stop Telling Women They Have Imposter Syndrome." *Harvard Business Review*, February 11, 2021.

theme for the remainder of high school and beyond. I had a nagging fear of never being good enough, not just in Mrs. H's class but in all classes, in every sport I played, and even in developing new friendships. I second-guessed every interaction. Am I being judged? Can I do this? Will they like me? Do I belong? Throughout high school, I experienced the "4 Ps of Imposter Syndrome": People Pleasing, Perfectionism, Paralysis, and Procrastination, [1] leading to a constant need for approval while impeding growth, innovation, and achievement. Deep down in my soul, I knew I was competent and deserving. But with little to no perceived support at school, I consistently allowed my inner saboteur to win, and I eventually fell from an exemplary student to an average one.

Upon sharing this revelation, I feel compelled to retire my usage of the term *imposter syndrome*. I rebuke the victimizing experience and choose instead to focus on a journey of growth and empowerment, emphasizing the positive aspects of overcoming challenges. As of today, I replace the terminology *"suffering from imposter syndrome"* with *"experiencing a Self-Perception Evolution"*™.

When experiencing a self-perception evolution, we should analyze the negative impacts of our delayed action. I had a client working three jobs and struggling to make ends meet. She was offered an opportunity to meet with a senior executive at a prestigious company and discuss a potential new role that could double her total salary. The client contemplated not having the conversation because external voices and inner saboteurs convinced her she wasn't worthy of the opportunity. Fortunately, coaching and therapy prevailed, and she landed that job with a 276% salary increase! Is your potential gain louder than those internal or external voices?

---

[1]Cashin, Lis. "The 4 P's of Imposter Syndrome and how They Impact Women Leaders." LinkedIn. November 9, 2023. https://www.linkedin.com/pulse/4-ps-imposter-syndrome-how-impact-women-leaders-lis-cashin-kvhre/.

## Impact on Mental Health

Imposter syndrome is just the tip of the iceberg when discussing the psychological tolls of stereotyping and bias. Not only can the cumulative experiences of subtle discrimination impede personal and professional growth, but workplace trauma can contribute to feelings of isolation, stress, depression, anxiety, and other mental health challenges.

Deloitte's study highlights the adverse impacts of covering an employee's well-being, purpose, and authenticity. Employees reported being "emotionally drained, feeling a need to mirror the behaviors and appearances of those with favored identities to be perceived as more professional, and experiencing a negative impact on their commitment to their organization."[1]

On the very day I reviewed this chapter with my publisher, Lincoln University administrator Antoinette "Bonnie" Candia-Bailey experienced the most tragic effect of workplace trauma. Feeling depressed and unsupported at work, rebuffed by board members when she asked for help, bullied, and fired by her boss, Bonnie felt the only recourse was to take her life.[2] Listen, if you haven't ever heard this from anyone else: You *deserve* to work in a psychologically safe space. To thrive, not barely survive, you must shift your mindset from tolerance to self-advocacy and empowerment.

## Strategies to Overcome Stereotypes and Biases

1.  Create Awareness. Leverage opportunities to educate on diversity, cultural competency, and psychological safety within the corporate culture. Influence and promote training programs to help employees

---

[1] "New Deloitte Study Reveals Most US Workers 'Cover' Their Identities at Work to Their — And Their Employers'— Detriment." Deloitte.

[2] "Historically Black Missouri College in Turmoil After Suicide of Administrator Who Alleged Bullying." *USNews.Com* (Jefferson City), January 19, 2024. https://www.usnews.com/news/us/articles/2024-01-19/historically-black-missouri-college-in-turmoil-after-suicide-of-administrator-who-alleged-bullying.

recognize and address microaggressions, understand cultural nuances, and reduce biases, fostering a more inclusive and respectful workplace. Embrace authenticity in modeling "uncovering" and encourage leaders and peers to do the same in your quest to disrupt cover culture.

2. Analyze Existing Organizational Policies. Propose improvements to address microaggressions. This may include implementing reporting mechanisms, conducting regular diversity and inclusion training, and establishing a zero-tolerance policy for discrimination.

3. Form or Join Workplace Support Networks and Affinity Groups. Connect with a community because shared experiences can often provide emotional support and additional coping strategies. Leverage mentorship relationships and alliances that can offer guidance and support during difficult times.

4. Recognize the Importance of Coaching, Mentorship, and Sponsorship Programs. Having trusted advisors externally and within the organization's leadership is essential for career advancement. However, not all your advocates will match your social identities. Expand your network to include cheerleaders, allies, and challengers who will have your back as you navigate the corporate landscape. Don't forget to pay it forward as you ascend into leadership.

5. Practice Empowerment and Self-Advocacy. Assert yourself as you communicate but be sure to maintain boundaries. Teach people how to treat you and don't compromise on your values. Cultivate the ability to express yourself confidently while actively listening to ensure your voice is heard.

6. Develop a Growth Mindset. Embrace challenges and setbacks as opportunities for learning and personal development rather than insurmountable obstacles.

Be open to change and proactively seek growth opportunities. Don't be afraid to ask for help.
7. Prioritize Self-Care. Taking care of yourself mentally, physically, spiritually, is critical in sustaining mental and emotional well-being. Explore mindfulness, stress management, and maintaining a healthy work-life balance to cope with the pressures of corporate life. Your job should *never* eclipse your physical and mental health. Let's normalize taking a mental health day or getting therapy.
8. Set Realistic and Achievable Goals. Get into the habit of breaking your goals into smaller, more manageable tasks to maintain motivation and a sense of accomplishment.
9. Remember to Celebrate Your Successes, No Matter How Small! Recognize and reward yourself for personal and professional achievements. Doing so contributes to a positive mindset and reinforces resilience.

## CONCLUSION

In environments where we're told to "bring your authentic self" (but not too much), acknowledging the implications of stereotypes and biases and embracing strategies for overcoming them is critical to career success. We must recognize negative workplace behaviors when they occur and take steps to mitigate the adverse physical and mental health effects. In the next chapter, Xenia Barnes explores this as well as authenticity in the workplace.

In concluding this chapter, I want to acknowledge the personal resilience and inner strength my fellow marginalized corporate professionals must often summon. In this context, I find a profound sense of solace and empowerment in one of the first songs I learned as a child, "This Little Light of Mine."

Its simple yet profound lyrics resonate deeply with the journey of anyone who has ever felt overshadowed or undervalued in a corporate setting. Just as this song has historically inspired individuals to stand against injustice and assert their rightful place in the world, it has also been a source of personal inspiration in the workplace, encouraging me not only to recognize my value but also to shine brightly even in environments that may not be designed for my success.

As we move forward, I encourage you to incorporate the message of this song into your professional lives, displaying your unique talents and perspectives with pride. Let's continue challenging biases and stereotypes for ourselves and those who will follow. Each of us has a light to shine—a distinct contribution to make—and in the face of challenges, we should never let anyone, or any environment, snuff out that light.

> *This little light of mine,*
> *I'm gonna let it shine.*
> *Let it shine,*
> *let it shine,*
> *let it shine.*

—Harry Dixon Loes

---

**Glynnis E. Swan**
Glynnis E. Swan has leveraged 18+ years of experience and credentials in HR and Global Talent Mobility to support and empower diverse companies and communities. She is passionate about advancing DEI agendas within the global HR industry and beyond, and her efforts have earned recognition as a 2023 Global Mobility Top 100 Diversity Champion. As an agent of change, she always seeks the next practice, not just the best practice, to create a positive and lasting impact.

# 3

# THE INVISIBLE TRENCH

## My Story from the Frontlines of Urban Education

### Dr. Carrie Young-McWilliams

*You can't teach what you don't know, and you can't lead where you won't go.*
—Dr. Carrie Young McWilliams

(I wrote that on a Post-it and stuck it to my laptop the year I almost walked away.)

### The Calling

I stepped into my first classroom at 24—freshly married to a deployed submariner, clutching a baby monitor in one hand and a curriculum guide in the other. My classroom was on the first floor of a school named for the first Black teacher in the school district the heart of the city's urban core. Located right next to the district central offices.

But my kids? They were alive—loud, hungry, and brilliant a mix of Black, Dominican, and Puerto Rican heritage. I wasn't just teaching 6th grade English and social studies. I was teaching survival. I was teaching identity. I taught through the textbook and into the trauma.

I stayed late. Brought snacks. Called parents on my commute. Showed up at football games, quinceanera and funerals. I taught the Sharon Drapers collection right next to the old English Classic that were mandated. I swapped "What's your thesis?" for "What's your truth?"

And the more I poured, the more my white colleagues pulled. They could not understand why I cared so much and why my students and parents cared so much for me.

## The Distancing

At first, it was subtle. No one sat with me in staff lunches, mainly because I would not speak negatively about students. My classroom ideas were "too radical" or "not data-driven." My mentorship of my melanated students was labeled "favoritism." My parent outreach was considered "overstepping."

I was one of six Black staff members in a building of nearly 100. Not just the youngest. I was the only Black woman with her eyes on a doctorate degree. The only one with a baby strapped to my chest during PD days. The only one who knew what it meant to code-switch in the teacher's lounge.

I tried potlucks. I tried small talk. I tried mirroring their tone, their humor, their distance. But the more I leaned in, the more they leaned out.

## The Invisible Trench

I first heard the term "mob mentality" in a Saturday leadership cohort. My professor, a Black woman from Boston, looked us dead in the eyes and said, "Mob mentality in education is when a group of educators—often white, often tenured—collectively isolate, undermine, or sabotage a Black educator who threatens the status quo. It's not always loud. It's silence in meetings. It's whispers in the hallway. It's your name left off the agenda. It's your presence policed."[1] I felt that in my bones.

I had become a threat—not because I was wrong, but because I was different. Because I knew the research. Because I named the bias. Because I refused to teach compliance over liberation.

## THE STRATEGY

I stopped trying to be liked. I started trying to be effective.

| Traditional Path | My Path |
|---|---|
| Wait for approval | *Create my own table* |
| Ask for leadership | *Build leadership* |
| Seek inclusion | *Build infrastructure* |

I became:

- Saturday School Director I turned the cafeteria into a liberation lab, having my students write

---

[1] James, L. (2019). The Pedagogy of Punishment: How Schools Eat Their Young. Journal of Black Educator Resistance, 12(3), 45–62.

produce and perform the first stage play about the life of Bennie Dover Jackson.
- Department Chair – I rewrote the curriculum to include culturally relevant text, spoken word, and restorative justice.
- Graduate Student – again. Not just to rise, but to understand the system that kept trying to erase me.

I asked for feedback—from the right people:
- Two Black principals with longstanding community ties.
- A Latina superintendent in Phoenix.
- A white co-worker and graduate classmate, Michelle, an ally who didn't flinch when I said, "I think I'm being sabotaged."

They told me, "You're not crazy. You're just first. And first is lonely."

## The Mob Moves

The more I rose, the more the mob shifted.
- My observations were "too emotional."
- My data was "incomplete."
- My students' growth was "an anomaly."
- My leadership was "too fast."

- I was reported for "raising my voice" when holding those in my department accountable for doing their job.
- I was excluded from a district-wide curriculum team and professional trainings—after I wrote the proposal.

But I documented everything. I saved emails. I recorded meetings. I built a paper trail like a soldier builds a trench.

## THE COURSE CORRECTION

I didn't burn out. I burned in. I learned:
- To pause before reacting.
- To ask: "Is this about me or the system?"
- To find safe spaces...not comfortable ones.
- To mother myself the way I mothered my students.

I brought my daughter to allowed extracurricular events. I taught her how to read the room. I showed her that Black women can lead, cry, course-correct, and still rise.

## THE NEXT LEVEL

When I was finally promoted to assistant principal, I thought, "Maybe now I can breathe. Maybe now I can rest. Maybe now I can just be." But the next level was just a deeper trench.
- Now I was over the teachers who once shunned me.
- Now I was under the superintendent who praised me.
- Now I was between the board and the community—both watching.

The mob had just changed uniforms.

## THE LESSON

I didn't win the game. I learned the game. And then I rewrote the rules. I mentored the next me.

I told her:
"You are not too much. You are just enough.
You are not early. You are on time.

You are not alone. You are the first of many."

## CLOSING NOTE

"They thought they could freeze me out.
But I was never ice.
I was fire.
And fire doesn't beg for warmth.
It creates it."

—Me, in my journal, 2019

Dr. Carrie Young-McWilliams
www.care2empower.org
Dr. Carrie Young-McWilliams is a passionate advocate for social justice and educational equity from Mississippi, in Maryland. With a background deeply rooted in civil rights activism, Carrie brings extensive experience in educational leadership, having spearheaded transformative initiatives in low-performing high schools and led district-wide reform efforts. Carrie holds degrees from prestigious institutions such as the University of Central Florida, Sacred Heart University, and the University of Sarasota, where her doctoral research focused on student mobility. As the CEO of Young-McWilliams Education Consulting Services, LLC, she continues her mission to advance diversity, equity, inclusion, and justice (DEIJ) in education, all while proudly representing Delta Sigma Theta, Inc.

# 4

# AUTHENTIC SELF-EXPRESSION AS AN ACT OF REVOLUTION

## Dr. Xenia Barnes

She was heading my way, swirling the ends of her hair between her fingers as they so often do. My teeth clenched, and I mentally rolled my eyes, thinking, "Here comes the bulls**t!"

I had just left the school leadership meeting, and I only had 5 minutes before teachers would enter the room for the weekly professional development session. For three years, I worked on the school culture team, reporting to her. Our relationship was rocky, to say the least.

As she got closer, I smirked and slid on my invisible mask as the words came slithering out of "Karen's" privileged mouth. "Ms. Barnes, I somehow get the feeling that you just are not being your authentic self in the meetings." Oh, she tried it!

'B*tch, please!' echoed in my head as I felt steam rising through my body. Then I thought, "Well, look at Captain Obvious! Why would I give her access to my authentic self when she still hasn't increased my salary to match the brilliance I bring to every talk, meeting, professional development workshop, parent

30

conference—and let's not even get started on the infuriating refrain of 'Let's ask Ms. Barnes what Black parents need to discuss?' How racist! Did they really expect me to be the voice of every single Black parent whose children attended this school? Because that assumption set me off, I always held my breath and counted to 10 before responding, "How about we do a survey and ask parents for topics they'd be interested in, or maybe utilize the PTA to come up with ideas?"

So here she was with another racist comment. I counted to 10 to keep my cool and do my job, then swirled the ends of my hair between my fingers—just like she did—and smiled. "I guess we'll never know," and she walked away.

## THE AUTHENTICITY TRAP

In the past, I could never determine whether "showing up as your authentic self" was performative and part of a hidden corporate agenda against people of color. As I navigated 10 years of leadership roles as an educator, dean, and supervisor with gaslighting supervisors and workplace mobbing, the phrase triggers me today. It's a setup, y'all!

While I would have liked to believe Karen's request for me to show up authentically was coming from a place of caring and support, there are too many statistics that show otherwise. Research has consistently shown that Black job applicants with natural, African-style hair face more negative assessments by hiring managers, being perceived as more aggressive and less professional, which suggests the impact of racial prejudices on views of employment. [1] Black professionals also remain

---

[1] "Research Suggests Bias Against Natural Hair Limits Job Opportunities for Black Women." n.d. Duke's Fuqua School of Business.
https://www.fuqua.duke.edu/duke-fuqua-insights/ashleigh-rosette-research-suggests-bias-against-natural-hair-limits-job.

significantly more likely to be fired or laid off than their white colleagues in today's organizations.[1]

The consequences I immediately feared when she made that comment included losing my job, stalling my career progression, having innovative ideas ignored, and experiencing escalated microaggressions. So yeah. She tried it.

Both managers and employees understand the need to conceal our authentic selves, and statistics illustrate the dangers of asking for authenticity. A 2022 study published in the Journal of Applied Psychology found that people of color are more likely to hide their authentic selves to appear less different from white coworkers.[2] For Black people in the workplace, this often looks like code switching, wearing straight hair or a wig, and keeping silent about covert and overt racism in the workplace.

Here are a few reasons why we do it:

1. Fear of judgment. Judgments from colleagues can be intimidating and may jeopardize relationships necessary to get work done smoothly.

2. Lack of psychological safety. The inherent lack of trust and safe space to make mistakes compounds insecurities about freely discussing mental health struggles, disclosing disabilities requiring accommodations, or suggesting divergent ideas without ridicule.[3]

---

[1] Umoh, Ruth. 2024. "Newly Hired Black Workers Face Greater Scrutiny From Their Bosses, Study Finds." Fortune, January 31, 2024. https://fortune.com/2024/01/31/black-workers-new-hires-scrutiny-fired-unemployment/.

[2] Hewlett, Sylvia Ann. 2014. "Too Many People of Color Feel Uncomfortable at Work." Harvard Business Review. August 7, 2014. https://hbr.org/2012/10/too-many-people-of-color-feel#:~:text=Overall%2C%20people%20of%20color%20are,African%2DAmerican%20network%20TV%20manager.

[3] Henneborn, Laurie. 2021. "Make It Safe for Employees to Disclose Their Disabilities." Harvard Business Review. September 13, 2021. https://hbr.org/2021/06/make-it-safe-for-employees-to-disclose-their-disabilities.

3. Wanting to "fit in." Within the workplace, these often show up as hiding quirky passions, nerdy personality traits, introversion, or extroversion tendencies that could make us perceived us as misfits among our colleagues.
4. Imposter syndrome. An alarming number of professionals grapple with perpetual self-doubt in their capabilities or adequate performance to justify their roles. This foments imposter syndrome, causing intense psychological strain and a lack of trust in one's competence.
5. Risk of adverse impact. People conceal aspects of themselves to allay fears of losing out on leadership opportunities or even facing termination if these traits become public knowledge.

While this has been deemed a self-preservation strategy to navigate corporate America, it's taking a toll on our mental and physical health.

According to a recent Yale School of Medicine article, Black women experience sustained physiological challenges from navigating multiple forms of racism and sexism, which cause physiological deterioration or 'weathering' of the body at young ages."[1] Researchers found that by age 50, Black women show substantially higher levels of inflammation and regulation of over 100 genes associated with illnesses, comparable to white women who are 20 years older. This disproportionate physical stress contributes to high rates of chronic disease early in life.

Another study found evidence that Black men who experienced longer durations of economic hardship and

---

[1] Yup, Kayla. 2022. "Black Women Excluded From Critical Studies Due to 'Weathering.'" Yale School of Medicine. December 1, 2022. https://medicine.yale.edu/news-article/black-women-excluded-from-critical-studies-due-to-weathering/.

discrimination based on their race had a higher risk of early-onset chronic illness and aging-related cell changes compared to Black men without similar exposures.[1]

The cumulative toll of hiding our authentic selves to survive toxic work climates is real and destructive. As the research shows, the sustained stress of inauthenticity is taking a toll on our mental health, speeding our aging process, and causing disease. Though adaptations like code-switching or straightening hair might seem harmless, the underlying reason—to mitigate racism, sexism, and other prejudices—means these masking behaviors still exact a heavy price on our health and well-being.

## HOW AUTHENTICITY LOOKS

*Embrace the strength within your roots, for in the tapestry of self-identity, each* thread weaves a powerful narrative of resilience and pride.

—Coach Barnes

Developing a strong sense of self-identity and expanding self-awareness are key to minimizing the harmful effects of denying our authentic selves.

Self-identity determines our driving motivations and what we stand for at the core—summed up in what thought leaders often call your "why statement." It provides deeper wisdom around our needs, emotions, strengths, and desires to set healthy boundaries.

Fortifying self-awareness as a complement requires turning inward to recognize triggers, insecurities, communication styles, and emotional patterns. What specific situations reliably cue stress responses like fight-flight-freeze-fawn due to past

---

[1] Allen, Julie Ober, Daphne C. Watkins, Linda M. Chatters, Arline T. Geronimus, and Vicki Johnson-Lawrence. 2019. "Cortisol and Racial Health Disparities Affecting Black Men in Later Life: Evidence From MIDUS II." American Journal of Men's Health 13 (4): 155798831987096. https://doi.org/10.1177/1557988319870969.

wounds or trauma? How do compulsive over-apologizing or people-pleasing instincts signal lingering self-worth issues? By patiently exploring this through journaling or counseling, you gain the power to respond consciously rather than react unconsciously.

By working on both, you develop:

1. A clear self-identity. This leads to communication that is grounded in your core values, priorities, and sense of purpose, regardless of what's going on around you. When you have a solid inner foundation, you rely less on external cues about how to show up. This makes it easier to retain your authentic communication styles, hairstyles, etc., even when they go against workplace cultural norms.

2. Expanded self-awareness. Becoming more self-aware builds an understanding of what situations tap into your insecurities. You gain insight into moments and conversations when you feel most vulnerable to others' judgments or scrutiny. You can then anticipate these stressful situations and intentionally center yourself on self-compassion as a buffer.

3. Deeper knowledge of your emotional patterns. Strengthening your emotional intelligence helps you recognize early on when you have slipped into people-pleasing, masking, or hiding behaviors in hopes of securing approval or allaying judgment. This allows you to catch yourself over-adapting and course-correcting yourself so that you are in alignment with your identity and needs.

4. Authenticity, even in restrictive environments. As Brené Brown warns, the most dangerous ideologies package oppression as wisdom. Wisdom, however, comes from within and doesn't require external validation. Anchoring ourselves in our inner light enables us to clearly

evaluate situations and, as a result, move authentically.

I was working in an environment that sucked the warmth out of the building and the life out of my spirit. I felt defeated, tired, and lifeless. Karen—the comfort and authenticity police—was stealing the joy of coming to work and doing what I loved—working with children and families and shaping the minds of future leaders. Don't let anyone steal your joy.

For years, Karen and I were at odds on several issues. But it was this situation that motivated me to seek a better way of handling things. There were continuous meetings when my ideas were later stolen in front of my eyes—"Christina"Columbused—as if I could not distinguish my suggestions from a whitewashed paraphrase. I no longer found solace in being there. But I knew I had to determine what showing up and remaining true to myself meant. To do that, I had to determine what was more important to me: proving Karen wrong or doing my job.

Should I continue to focus my efforts on correcting my manager's problematic behaviors? Doing so only led to disagreements and tension. I wasn't getting anywhere. My other option was to focus on finding fulfillment in simply doing my job. I was in a career that I loved, and I couldn't imagine doing anything else. And I couldn't deny the impact we made on the students; I enjoyed talking with the parents, and I loved working in a predominantly Black school. I eventually realized that changing others was outside my control. Instead, I reclaimed my power by doing what she asked me to do—showing up authentically. By focusing inward, I developed a strong sense of self-identity and expanded my self-awareness. And when I did, I got my joy back.

The first thing I did was change how I communicated with Karen. Rather than offering my ideas freely only to have them disregarded and regurgitated, I shifted my approach. When Karen asked for suggestions, my new response was, "Why don't you share your ideas first, and we can build from there?" By stepping back as the idea generator, I regained authority over how I engaged.

Focusing my energy on fulfilling my professional responsibilities rather than seeking validation or attempting to change others' problematic behaviors was an empowering step towards authenticity. This act of focusing on my purpose as an educator working with children—my "why"—strengthened my self-identity. Rather than allowing external factors to steer my sense of purpose and joy, I reconnected with my internal motivations.

Focusing inward also enhanced my self-awareness. I gained clarity about boundaries and where I did and didn't have agency. I recognized that exerting efforts to change or convince my manager was an exercise in futility that drained my energy. This self-insight about my sphere of influence and control oriented my attention toward what I could impact. It also helped illuminate my emotional triggers. My experiences with having my ideas rejected or stolen touched on deeper wounds of invalidation and erasure. This made me more aware of my self-worth and helped me recognize that my voice was worth hearing. I started to advocate for myself and find ways to communicate without feeling powerless. I also became more aware of my interactions with others and the energy I brought to conversations. This paved the way for me to maintain my authentic self and find fulfillment even in an unsupportive environment. The journey of self-discovery gave me tools to define myself rather than be defined by others' limited perspectives.

Taking ownership of your self-identity and developing self-awareness are ongoing journeys that require dedication and courage. If you're facing a similar crossroads, ask yourself these reflective questions to bolster your sense of purpose and strengthen your knowledge of emotional patterns.

**Self-Identity**
1. What are your core values?
2. What is your purpose in life?
3. What is your plan for the future?
4. What principles do you stand by, no matter what?

**Self-Awareness**
1. Do you react to disappointment by addressing issues directly or deflecting pain?
2. Given what you know about stress now, what would you tell your younger self?
3. What boundaries or self-care habits could you implement to build resilience?
4. In what area do you need to grow emotionally the most?
5. How do you feel when faced with change?
6. Do you believe in giving second chances?
7. What is your greatest strength, and why?
8. How often do you ask others for help?

## THE CALL FOR AUTHENTICITY

*You've got to learn to leave the table when love's no longer being served.*

—Nina Simone

Karen and I continued to work together until she moved on to a new position. She was replaced by a dashiki-wearing Black woman. Ironically, she was mentally shackled to an oppressive mindset and operated just like Karen. And she ended up dismantling the last essence of Black community teachers and staff we had left. By that time, my illness had taken over, and I was no longer willing to allow the darkness of stress to penetrate my peace and mental well-being. For me, protecting my peace in the workplace meant knowing when to walk away.

As you embark on your workplace journey as a team member or leader, I offer the following advice: lead with love. When I started my coaching business, I was determined not to be the kind of leader I had encountered over the years. Thus, I grounded myself in the following principles: truth, peace, transparency, and balance. You can do the same wherever you work, in any job you perform.

Determine what each of the principles above means to you, or define your own. When you do, your vision of an authentic, peaceful leader will become clear. Then strive to live by those principles. Through them, you can create a culture that is based on trust and respect, where everyone is valued and can thrive. Remember:

People feel comfortable being themselves in a peaceful work environment based on trust and respect. People can share ideas openly without fear of judgment or retaliation when there is less conflict, drama, or politics. This supports authentic self-expression.

People tend to perceive leaders who cultivate a calm and understanding work culture as more genuine and sincere. If leaders have open communication, admit mistakes, listen to feedback, and prioritize employee well-being, people are more likely to view them as authentic. Again, as a leader, you will need to determine what this looks and feels like for the workplace culture you are aiming to build.

Companies that value work-life balance, diversity, and inclusion help employees integrate their personal and professional identities. Policies that support employees' physical and emotional needs allow people to show up more fully as themselves without feeling the need to compartmentalize different aspects of self.

Workplaces characterized by psychological safety, where people aren't afraid to take interpersonal risks, create environments where employees can share their true perspectives easier. Feeling assured that your vulnerabilities won't be held against you promotes authentic conversations.

Non-hierarchical workplaces with collaborative norms can foster authenticity by valuing all voices equally. When decisions are made democratically and ideas can come from anyone, people are empowered to contribute in their authentic way.

The journey to embracing authenticity in the workplace is complex and ongoing. Yet, we can cultivate genuine self-expression by growing our self-knowledge and centering our inner light to navigate repressive spaces. As leaders, we shape the path ahead through the cultures we create and the norms we challenge. And being authentic means that staff can stand fully for who they are. My hope is that we each find fulfillment and purpose while bringing our complete selves to uplift our teams and organizations. The world needs the full measure of our collective brilliance.

**Dr. Xenia Barnes, M.Ed, CHRC**
www.xeniabarnes.com
Dr. Xenia Barnes leverages behavioral analysis and community activism experience as a dynamic speaker, author, and trauma coach transforming domestic abuse, gun violence, and illness survivors. A PhD candidate, her acclaimed talk inspires audiences on loving themselves through trauma. Her coaching polishes inner gems so teams can enhance performance via strategic thinking, smart management, efficient planning, and essential training.

# 5

# A JEDI WARRIOR
# LEADS WITH GRACE

## Dr. Tauheedah Baker-Jones

*Education either functions as an instrument that is used to facilitate integration of the younger generation into the logic of the present system and bring about conformity to it, or it becomes the practice of freedom, the means by which men and women deal critically and creatively with reality and discover how to participate in the transformation of their world.*

—Paulo Regulus Freire

Let me take you on a journey that began during my senior year at UCLA. Back then, my plans were clear: I was headed to Divinity School. But everything changed when I enrolled in a course titled "The Politics of Education." It was in this class that I first encountered the powerful ideas of Paulo Freire and the profound impact that education could have on shaping a better world.

Aristotle once stated that "Where the needs of the world and your talents cross, there lies your vocation." In that transformative semester, I realized that education would become the way that I would put my faith into action. I also realized that education wasn't just about passing on knowledge; it was a tool for liberation. It was also the means, by which, we could ensure that demography did not dictate destiny for children. That's when I made the pivotal decision to dedicate my life to this cause—to become a champion of education as a practice of freedom, as Freire so eloquently put it, and I committed the next 20+ years of my life to engaging in a practice that Freire describes as "reflection and action directed at systems to be transformed."

## A MISSION TO TRANSFORM SYSTEMS

My journey as a JEDI (Justice, Equity, Diversity, and Inclusion) leader began with a clear mission: to transform systems and ensure equitable access to quality education for all children. Thus, I took on the role of Chief Equity and Social Justice Officer at a major school district in the Southeast, fully aware of the challenges that lay ahead. I was stepping into uncharted territory as the district's first equity leader, the first female district equity leader in the state, and at a time of national racial unrest and political polarization.

Despite the complexities that I was stepping into, I saw immense promise in the district's commitment to equity. They had recently passed a robust equity policy, unveiled a comprehensive five-year strategic plan, and appointed a superintendent explicitly committed to advancing equity. In addition, I was told that I would be a member of the Superintendent's Senior Cabinet, involved in all major district decisions (academics, finance, operations, talent management, and stakeholder engagement). It was also shared with me that I was hired for the role because I had the depth of experience and expertise that they needed, I was also courageous and bold, and I was eagerly ready to challenge the status quo. With a sufficient budget, philanthropic support, and the potential to impact thousands of families, I believed that if this work couldn't happen here, it couldn't happen anywhere..

## UNFORESEEN CHALLENGES

*We can, whenever we choose, teach all children whose learning is important to us. Whether we do so depends upon how we feel about the fact that we have not done so already.*

—Dr. Ron Edmunds

When I accepted the role of Chief Equity and Social Justice Officer, I had high hopes and a clear sense of purpose. I quickly came to understand that, despite my position, I truly had very little influence over shaping large-scale decisions and organizational strategy. It also didn't take long for me to realize that my role had been haphazardly conceived and that the organization was unclear about its expectations around my body of work.

When it came to leading the JEDI work, while my experience and expertise were acknowledged, my advice and insights were often dismissed or unwelcome. Despite being hired for my eagerness and courage, I frequently found my passion mislabeled as anger or bossiness, and my zeal mislabeled as intimidation. Challenging the status quo and dominant culture, a fundamental aspect of my job, was met with resistance, punishment, and accusations of being "difficult," "not a team player," and "out for myself." These same peers also refused to do the reflective work to unpack the bias and internalized oppression inherent in their characterizations, even when other colleagues, who took the time to meaningfully work with and get to know me, characterized me as otherwise. As a result, I became the recipient of a steady stream of micro- and macro-aggressions, and the sweeping negative characterizations undermined my efforts.

Meanwhile, the organization's resistance to collaboration became increasingly evident. To avoid my challenge and candor, I was frequently cut out of key meetings, data and information were hoarded from me and my team, and any attempt to measure anything of substance was met with willful resistance (active and passive). Moreover, the level of consensus-building that was needed to establish a foundation for the changes we were championing demanded a level of mental agility and fortitude that was unsustainable.

Working in the South brought an additional layer of challenges. I had to contend with threatening letters and phone calls from external constituents who were against all forms of JEDI work, while also dealing with the internal resistance. In addition, I was subjected to a venomous brand of workplace mobbing. [1] which caused me to become the social media target of false accusations and character assassinations by an anonymous group of individuals working silently with co-workers to remove me, dismantle my team, and reset the status quo.

My job became a daily battle to do the work I was hired to do. While I had expected some resistance, the extent of the pushback I encountered was disheartening. I spent much of my time strategizing how to circumvent the resistance to move the work forward. Indeed, it was a challenging paradox to navigate— to be both the disruptor and the one being disrupted. I felt my passion being drained day by day. Despite this, I remained thoughtful, poised, and grounded in grace, coaching and counseling my team, while nursing my own wounds.

What I can say about my experience with this organization, is that it was indeed the hardest role I have ever taken. It required me to show up in a manner unlike any other leadership role I had ever taken on. It also came at a great cost to my physical health, mental well-being, and professional reputation. Nonetheless, my approach to the work was grounded in two pivotal understandings that supported my success and longevity in the role.

The first is that many who undermined and resisted our JEDI efforts were themselves victims of the culture we aimed to change. Paradoxically, many of them genuinely supported advancing JEDI within our organization. However, they failed to

---

[1] Gillette, H. (2022, July 21). Mobbing at work: signs and effects of group bullying. Psych Central. https://psychcentral.com/health/mobbing-at-work-group-bullying

implicate themselves in both the problem and the solution. As a result, they couldn't see when their actions were problematic or how they aligned with the prevailing culture of marginalization that they had internalized.

These individuals also failed to reflect on their internalized oppression, neglecting to realize how their behaviors—power hoarding, conflict avoidance, defensiveness, skepticism, and equity washing—upheld the dominant culture and perpetuated institutional oppression and marginalization.[1] As shared, they attributed the organization's JEDI challenges to the actions of others and never saw themselves as part of the problem or the solution. This understanding allowed me to extend grace to those resistant to change. In order to do so successfully, I challenged my team and I to meet them where they were and admit that, like all of us, they were products of the culture we were trying to change. Dr. Tanji Reed-Marshall's statement about protecting autonomy and power resonated deeply in my experience. She stated that "a fine line separates working to protect your autonomy to make critical educational decisions on behalf of your students and working to protect the power your autonomy offers.[2]

In addition to realizing the paradox above, I also came to understand that, those who championed our work, underestimated what it truly takes to change a culture of institutional oppression and marginalization. When we pushed against the system, the status quo snapped back twice as hard. Therefore, it was necessary for me to help my JEDI champions understand that true JEDI work is a long game of chess, not checkers. Consequently, we created an underground network of co-conspirators and allies who supported us in moving the work. I also developed two frameworks to guide my team's efforts and safeguard our success. These frameworks allowed us to triumph in

---

[1] Dismantling Racism & White Supremacy Culture: A Workbook for Social Change Groups, by Kenneth Jones and Tema Okun, ChangeWork, 2001

[2] Marshall, T. R. (2023). *Understanding your instructional power, curriculum and language decisions to support each student*. ASCD.

the trenches despite the massive opposition to our work. As a result, within three years, we successfully positioned the organization as an award-winning, national model for intentionally and explicitly addressing challenges to equity in education. Here's how we did it:

## Two Frameworks for Success

As a leader, you must possess a great deal of professional agility to be successful. Each role and context requires something different from us and we must show up accordingly. How I showed up as the Chief Equity and Social Justice Officer was the result of the work that I was called there to do, and as shared, I showed up differently in that role than I had in any of my other roles before it because the position necessitated it for success.

To navigate the challenges I faced, I developed two frameworks for leading JEDI and any controversial transformative work effectively and within an accelerated timeline. Both were born out of necessity—a survival strategy to move the work forward and make a lasting impact. I call the first one the Lead with GRACE Framework, and GRACE is an acronym for Grace (for oneself and others), Reflection, Awareness (internal and external), Candor, and Empathy. This was the framework that I used as the primary lead for the JEDI work to successfully provide strategic leadership and guidance over the implementation of the district's vision and strategy for JEDI-focused change efforts. I also trained my team on using a second framework that I developed, known as the AMPLIFY Your Impact Framework. The AMPLIFY Your Impact Framework guided my team through a comprehensive process of Assessing, Mapping, Planning, Legitimizing, Iterating, Flexibility, and communicating our success (Yay!).

Each element of these frameworks contains a series of sub-frameworks that, when applied together, support the successful execution of any change effort. The Leading with GRACE Framework is one that I use to coach and develop JEDI leaders. The AMPLIFY Your Impact Framework is used to support teams leading large-scale change of any nature. To learn more about these frameworks, please email info@trinitystrategy.org. In this chapter, however, I will introduce you to the Grace (for oneself and others) and Empathy elements of the Lead with GRACE Framework.

## EXTENDING GRACE TO ONESELF

Extending grace to oneself was an essential part of the framework. In extending grace to yourself, it is important that you have a firm understanding of the identities that undergird your reason for doing JEDI work. To map my identities, I used Ronald Heifetz's Adaptive Leadership Framework and placed my identities into categories of Level I and Level II.[1] I also needed to manage and negotiate my Level I (Professional Identities) and Level II (Social Identities) identities appropriately to respond effectively in challenging situations.

Given the racially charged climate in which I entered my role, some of the most poignant identities that played into my ability to exercise leadership as an explicit JEDI leader included:

Level I (Professional Identities): JEDI Warrior: This identity was frequently used as a means of "work avoidance" for colleagues who preferred that I serve as the main advocate for JEDI concerns and/or who did not understand the necessity of building their own stamina for leading JEDI work. These colleagues would often rely solely on me to address issues of inequity and would be the ones to come to me after meetings, praising me for speaking up, and sharing a concern that they too had. Trying to convince these colleagues that initiating courageous conversations on JEDI was a shared responsibility often proved challenging.

Level II (Social Identities): African American/Black American: My identity as an African American/Black American added another layer to my commitment to my work. I was well-

---

[1] Heifetz, R. A., Linsky, M., & Grashow, A. (2017). The Practice of Adaptive Leadership Tools and Tactics for Changing Your Organization and the World. Boston: Harvard Business Review Press.

aware of the historical struggles faced by Black people in this country, and I felt a deep allegiance to this cause. Recent events of racial and civil unrest had only heightened the urgency of my work. People viewed my role as either a silver bullet to address these woes, or a silver bullet to end their privilege. This caused heightened tensions to become more pronounced and positioned me to be a professional martyr and scapegoat. Because of this, I was frequently triggered within meetings and worked diligently to balance my JEDI warrior tendencies to allow others to take on their share of ownership in the JEDI work.

Woman: As a woman in a highly patriarchal culture, I was frequently placed in a position where I was asked to explain my decision-making and justify my expertise. Speaking passionately about areas where the organization fell short of its stated values often resulted in harsh criticism. As a Black woman, these criticisms were even more pronounced. My passion was often mislabeled as anger, and my dedication was seen as intimidating or aggressive. Both came with dire professional consequences and damage to my professional reputation.

Perception Becomes Reality: When situations arose that triggered and activated one of the identities listed above, I asked critical questions and conducted internal scans to regulate my emotions, maintain composure, and make informed decisions. The questions that I asked as part of this internal scan come from the Heifetz Adaptive Leadership Framework and include:[1]

1. What identifications might have been activated and/or are relevant to this situation?
2. What assumptions—attitudes, beliefs, values, or sensitivities—have I internalized about what it means to be X in this situation?

---

[1] Heifetz, R. A., Linsky, M., & Grashow, A. (2017). *The Practice of Adaptive Leadership Tools and Tactics for Changing Your Organization and the World*. Boston: Harvard Business Review Press.

3. What expectations do I carry of myself from this/these relevant identity/identities? Are these expectations real or perceived?
4. Who do I believe I would disappoint if I behaved differently than my initial response or pattern in this situation? Is this disappointment real or perceived?
5. How might these help me in this situation? How might they be limiting me in this situation?
6. How should I guard against perceived expectations that may impede my ultimate goal or objective? How might I get in my own way?

This internal scan gave me the freedom I needed to respond appropriately in situations where tension and micro- and macro-aggressions were high. It also kept me empowered to give the work back to others, where it often belonged. Holding my identities as objects allowed me to renegotiate what it meant to be a social justice warrior, a Black American, and a Black woman. As a result, I was able to give myself the grace that I needed to intervene appropriately and move the work forward.

This internal scan gave me the freedom I needed to respond appropriately in situations where tension and micro- and macro-aggressions were high. It also kept me empowered to give the work back to others, where it often belonged. Holding my identities as objects allowed me to renegotiate what it meant to be a social justice warrior, a Black American, and a Black Woman. As a result, I was able to give myself the grace that I needed to intervene appropriately and move the work forward.

## WRAPPING GRACE IN A SCARF
*People don't fear change; they fear loss.*
—Dr. Danisa Amante-Jackson, Ed.L.D.

To support my team in holding grace for others, I would frequently remind them that people don't fear change; they fear loss. Because of this, they have an unconscious immune response to change that manifests as resistance. This message helped them understand the nature of the resistance and opposition we encountered and encouraged them not to take it personally. By extending grace, our JEDI work has made strides in promoting equity and inclusion within our organization.

The first step in cultivating a culture of grace for others was to hold a series of community conversations with internal and external stakeholders to learn and understand their hopes, fears, and apprehensions around the JEDI work that we were leading. These hopes, fears, and apprehensions provided insights into what the community and collective SCARF threats were and allowed us to proactively respond to these threats in a way that wasn't defensive but that garnered support or neutralized, to the greatest extent possible, resistance.

The concept of SCARF Threats was developed by David Rock, and in 2008 in his paper "SCARF: A Brain-Based Model for Collaborating With and Influencing Others."[1]

SCARF, an acronym representing five crucial "domains," plays a significant role in shaping our behavior within social contexts. These domains encompass status, certainty, autonomy, relatedness, and fairness, each acting as fundamental stimuli that can elicit either a "threat or reward" response. These five stimuli encompass the following aspects:

- Status: the perceived importance of an individual in comparison to others and their sense of self-worth.
- Certainty: the ability to anticipate future events with minimal surprises.
- Autonomy: the capacity to exert control over oneself and events.
- Relatedness: a feeling of connection and security in relation to others.

---

[1] Rock, D. (2008). 'SCARF: A Brain-Based Model for Collaborating With and Influencing Others,' *Neuroleadership Journal*, 1, 1-9.

- Fairness: the perception of an equitable and just environment.

When a person perceives a threat within any of these domains, their brain triggers a survival response. Consequently, when someone senses a social threat, their ability to think rationally or absorb new information also becomes impaired. Recognizing and responding to these factors can facilitate more adept leadership, influence, and collaboration.

Given that these threats are perception-based, an event that may seem innocuous or inconsequential to one individual could trigger a survival response in another. Therefore, when assuming JEDI leadership, it is crucial to strategize and create opportunities to bolster individuals' sense of belonging, autonomy, self-worth, or status while also building trust through consistency and fairness.

The community conversations illuminated for us what SCARF threats existed within our organization and within each of the communities that we served. What we learned is that majority communities typically had Status, Certainty, and Autonomy threats, whereas minority and historically marginalized communities tended to have Relatedness and Fairness threats. This information allowed us to develop a strategy to mitigate against this in our work, and we used the following chart in Exhibit 1 to craft communications and strategic actions accordingly:

## Exhibit 1: David Rock's SCARF Model[1]

**The SCARF Model**

| S Status | C Certainty | A Autonomy | R Relatedness | F Fairness |
|---|---|---|---|---|
| Looks at the relative importance of people | Looks at our ability to predict the future. How certain are we? | Looks at our perception of having control over our environment | Looks at our relationships and sense of fitting in | Looks at our perception of being treated fairly for you and for others |
| 'I am valuable' | 'I know where I stand or what will happen' | 'I have a choice' | 'I belong' | 'I am treated fairly and others are treated fairly' |

**What I Should Consider**

| | | | | |
|---|---|---|---|---|
| How can I ensure that they know they are valued? | How can I clarify where they stand and what will happen? | How can I provide them with some degree of input and choice? | How can I make them feel like part of the team? | Taking everything together, am I treating them and others fairly? |

## EMPATHY REQUIRES US TO BE BRAVE

JEDI work is fundamentally rooted in recognizing humanity in both ourselves and others. It acknowledges that our experiences shape our perceptions and that we are all products of the systems of inequity that surround us. Despite receiving implicit bias training and becoming aware of these biases, it's an ongoing daily practice to ensure they don't hinder our ability to show up as our best selves. Imperfection is inherent in our humanity, which is why the core value of my JEDI work is grace—extending it to both ourselves and others.

As a JEDI leader, I firmly believe in going easier on people and harder on systems. For me, this was done first by conducting empathy interviews with a cross-section of stakeholders upon entering my role. These interviews delved into personal and professional aspects and asked about their perceptions of equity, social justice, and the organization's racial equity agenda. This process allowed me to connect with stakeholders on a deeper level, understanding their personal experiences, histories, and

---

[1] Mind Tools. 2025. "David Rock's SCARF Model." Www.mindtools.com. 2025. https://www.mindtools.com/akswgc0/david-rocks-scarf-model.

worldviews. During the interviews, I asked, "I am interested in learning about you personally and professionally, what would you like me to know?" "What does equity mean to you?" "What does social justice mean for our organization?" "How would you describe the racial equity agenda of the organization?" "Does this work, related to equity, make sense for our organization at this time?" "In what way do you foresee the district's equity efforts impacting your child, the community, and/or your work?"

The insights gained from the empathy interviews also became the foundation for holding grace and empathy throughout my tenure in the organization. To cultivate a culture of empathy throughout the organization, I developed the BRAVE Discussion Framework for us to use when having difficult, controversial, or courageous conversations. This framework aimed to create brave spaces for critical dialogue, with BRAVE standing for:

B - Build coalitions across lines of difference and engage diverse voices and viewpoints.

R - Reserve judgment, be curious about intent, and challenge your assumptions.

A - Acknowledge the impact of statements and actions on others.

V - Value vulnerability, empathize with diverse experiences, and hold space for divergent truths.

E - Enthusiastically champion equity and reflect on opportunities for growth.

Embracing the BRAVE framework allowed us to engage in critical, and often triggering, dialogue while remaining self-reflective, self-accountable, and open to new perspectives. We complemented this framework with a centering protocol adapted from Chicago Public Schools.[1] This protocol consisted of three steps:

Step 1: Acknowledge the aspects of the BRAVE Discussion Framework that are challenging you at the moment.

---

[1] Chicago Public Schools "Equity CURVE." https://www.cps.edu/sites/equity/equity-framework/equity-in-cps/equity-curve.

Allow yourself the space to acknowledge your disposition and emotions.

Step 2: Identify aspects of the BRAVE Discussion Framework that can counter what's challenging you. Select a key phrase from the BRAVE Discussion Framework and repeat it twice. The first time is to acknowledge your disposition. The second time is to ground yourself. Use this affirmation to center yourself and anchor the comments you will share moving forward.

Step 3: Repeat Steps 1 and 2 as needed throughout the discussion, focusing on different elements of the BRAVE Discussion Framework.

This combination of the BRAVE framework, coupled with the centering protocol, allowed us to engage in challenging conversations in an empathetic and compassionate manner while also preserving the dignity and humanity of all involved.

## THE SACRIFICE FOR JUSTICE, EQUITY, DIVERSITY, AND INCLUSION

*Progress is a nice word. But change is its motivator. And change has its enemies.*

—Robert Kennedy

In the faith that I subscribe to, there is a quote that says, "Forgive them, Father, for they know not what they do." Throughout my journey as a JEDI leader, I would often have to remind myself of this to hold grace and space for people's unconscious biases, internalized oppression, and the trauma they would inflict on me because of their immunity to change.

What I took away from this experience is that when you are explicitly leading an organization's JEDI efforts, you are in a "kill the messenger" role. Quite honestly, if you're doing JEDI work and no one is angry, you're not truly doing JEDI work. The position requires you to shine a light on the inequitable practices that were inherent in the organization's deliberations, cultural practices, and actions. This creates a great deal of discomfort and tension for those around you. This is a consequence of the position, and it's the stance that you are required to take if you are to be successful in the role. This paradox wears on you mentally, emotionally and spiritually, and the hostile environment that it creates places you in a defensive and defenseless stance.

By leaning into this work, you sacrifice your professional reputation and develop strained relationships with your superiors and peers. People often have a hard time differentiating your push and passion for the work from your presence as a person and as a leader. You are repeatedly placed in positions where you have to sacrifice yourself and be subject to trauma. This is why the tenure of people in JEDI roles is so short, and those of us working within the system to bring about change must accept that the work has an abbreviated shelf life.

## CONCLUSION: WHEN IT'S OVER, IT'S OVER

When I first stepped into my role as a JEDI leader, a seasoned veteran in the field shared a piece of wisdom that has resonated with me throughout my journey. He advised me to write my letter of resignation immediately after signing my offer letter. This startling counsel was rooted in his own decade-plus experience in JEDI leadership. He had learned that a time would come when the organization would place me in a moral quandary, where I'd have to choose between walking away or becoming complicit in causing harm to others.

I'll never forget the day that moment arrived. It struck me like a tidal wave, overwhelming my heart. In response, I abruptly walked out of the meeting, retreated to my office, and dissolved into tears. Subsequently, I began succession planning, as I intended to step down within a year. I did not heed the elder's counsel to leave immediately. Instead, I considered my team and the fact that our work hadn't yet been integrated into the organization to ensure its longevity. I also considered my supervisor, who had created my role, and the repercussions my resignation might have on her. I thought about everyone and everything, except myself, and failed to heed the words of wisdom I was given.

My failure to prioritize my own well-being had grave consequences. My mental, physical, and emotional health deteriorated. In addition, opponents of the administration gradually gained influence, exerting pressure on the board to terminate my supervisor's tenure. Eventually, they won out and her successor swiftly diminished the JEDI office's positional power and influence by abolishing the Chief Officer's role, shuttering the Center for Equity and Social Justice, and downsizing and disbanding my team.

What I hope that you take away from this testimony is that no JEDI leader will ever be fully successful. I once read that JEDI work is a moving target, so the best any leader can do is to leave an organization better than how they found it. The real goal of this work is to aim for progress, and I had indeed made substantial progress during my time as a JEDI leader. Despite the challenges throughout my JEDI leadership journey, my path was also filled with triumphs.

As you embark on your own journey in this challenging but vital field, remember that this role demands self-awareness, resilience, and unwavering commitment to a higher purpose: the pursuit of a more just and equitable world. It is also important to remember that no one person can change culture and undo decades of institutional harm. It is ultimately the responsibility of the organization to address and undo the trauma it causes. Nonetheless, one person can make a difference, take up space, and be heard. Most importantly, remember that you are not alone. There is a whole army of JEDI warriors in the trenches fighting with you.

**Dr. Tauheedah Baker-Jones**
www.trinitystrategy.org
Dr. Tauheedah Baker-Jones is a dynamic systems leader with 20 years of experience ensuring an excellent learning environment for every child. In 2023, Dr. Baker-Jones received the Council of the Great City Schools District Equity Leader Award. In 2022, she was named as one of the Top 50 Women Leaders of Georgia by Women We Admire Magazine. Her personal motto is Dare to Be Bold, Your Best, & The Change!

# 6

# FIGHTING CORPORATE STYLE
## Applied Lessons from the Street

PHILLIP WOOLFOLK

Growing up on the rough side of the tracks, I remember fighting many of the bullies in the neighborhood. What I didn't know back then was how relevant those experiences would be to my future. My ability to assert myself, resist intimidation, and face my fears would prove to be a valuable asset and mindset in both the streets and corporate suites.

For openers, I remember one executive who thought raising his voice was going to intimidate me. I smiled at him and said, "You know, when you have had guns in your face and knives pulled on you, someone yelling is so far away from intimidating that you should lower your voice and have a seat before you give yourself a heart attack. Yelling at me is a real waste of your time, and I do not respond to it because you are not talking to me in that tone." I said it quietly and calmly, without flinching, with solid eye contact, and he left my office.

Nearly 70% of Americans are familiar with the concept of workplace bullying, while 19% have seen it happen and 30% have been the target of such treatment.[1] The incidence of bullying in the workplace was higher among African Americans compared to other racial groups.[2] Therefore, Black professionals are more likely to suffer from the effects of workplace bullying. Also, African Americans reported feeling more isolated at work, and workplace discrimination is also more prevalent among Black professionals. This suggests a lack of workplace support for African Americans, leading to an increase in workplace bullying. Additionally, this lack of support is a sign of a larger culture of discrimination in the workplace.[3]

As I share my stories of triumph, I will also share my background and personal experiences. At the time, I did not realize how all of it would prepare me for life in general and my corporate journey in particular. Let me start with one of my first corporate experiences which involved working at a bank that ultimately underwent acquisition during my seventh year of employment. This experience taught me that decisions were business and not personal.

So, take this journey with me. I started this job as a teller at the age of 20, and approximately seven years later, the bank was acquired. I had worked my way up from teller to foreign teller to assistant head teller, and I was a branch sales manager at the time of the acquisition. In this role, I was typically one of the top three sales reps, battling for the number one spot each month. Then, the acquiring bank came in and cut the incentivized compensation. They just got rid of the commission structure. I couldn't believe it!

[1]Yamada, D. n.d. "The Complete Report." Workplace Bullying Institute. Accessed January 22, 2024. https://workplacebullying.org/wp-content/uploads/2021/04/2021-Full-Report.pdf.
[2] Attell, Brandon K., Kiersten Kummerow Brown, and Linda A Treiber, 2017. "Workplace bullying, perceived job stressors, and psychological distress: gender and race differences in the stress process", Social Science Research, 65:210-221. https://doi.org/10.1016/j.ssresearch.2017.02.001
[3] Weldon-Caron, Rachael, 2022. "Hrd: what can we do to create a more just society for african americans in the workplace?", New Horizons in Adult Education and Human Resource Development(4), 34:44-49. https://doi.org/10.1002/nha3.20369

After that acquisition and throughout the rest of my banking career, I carried an unsigned resignation letter in my briefcase. It kept me grounded in the fact that I was hired and compensated to do a job, and either party could terminate that relationship at any time for any reason. I also discovered that employers respected and compensated employees who took the risk of moving around. I decided it was respect and not likeability that ruled the day, and the former was more critical than the latter. I had learned the value of mutual respect on my neighborhood block so, when it came to the corporate world, I picked up on it quickly.

The new retail sales division leader invited all the sales representatives to the corporate executive dining room to have lunch and get acquainted. Another principle I learned in my neighborhood was that you should not take anything from anyone, and you should not let anyone take anything from you. So, during lunch, the leader went around the room asking for everyone's opinion about the acquisition and what their experience had been so far. I sat and listened. Most of my colleagues had cordial things to say about the company and how they looked forward to working for this larger organization with a broader reach and wider range of products and services.

When it was my turn, I had just one question. I asked, "Since the commission is being cut, are the sales representatives going to receive a raise in base compensation commensurate with their average commission? If not, it would be a serious pay cut for those of us who are producing." You could hear a pin drop.

It was, after all, what we all wanted to know. After a longer than necessary pause, he responded that he did not know and that he would have to check and get back to me. My street instincts decided instantly that he was a liar, and my best course of action would be to explore opportunities elsewhere. How could he not know?

The next day, the regional manager stopped by my office, and I asked him a simple question: Are you staying? He, too, gave a pregnant pause. In his case, I understood why he would not want to share his honest answer with a subordinate and potentially have that subordinate share that response with others.

But my instincts told me his answer was no, so I let him off the hook and added, "I understand." I floated my resume, and in about two to three weeks, I was hired at a higher pay rate, recapturing my lost commission in my new base pay with the potential of earning commission. I started the new position with a resignation letter in my briefcase, no personal items in my office: no plants, flowers, or family photos. Absolutely nothing but my briefcase. That kept my professional life in the banking world strictly business, and there was never any need to pack, as I was always ready to leave at a moment's notice.

At another point in my career, I managed sales and operations for low- and moderate-income residential mortgage lending. My team supported homeownership in low- and moderate-income communities throughout New Jersey, Pennsylvania, and Delaware. People weren't interested in focusing on this population in the early days of this position. There were those who thought low- and moderate-income people were not a good financial risk. With a great deal of work, we eventually structured a unified approach to create an income portfolio of profitable loans. It turns out that low- and moderate-income homebuyers who looked like me were a good risk after all, and a lending analysis showed that this portfolio was performing just as well as any other loan product group. Another triumph in the trenches!

After that success, I determined that the traditional mortgage banking group and the low- and moderate-income group should be combined. My position had become obsolete, and I shared my thoughts with my vice president at the time. I excelled at resolving issues, while his role involved identifying the next steps to take. Senior management concurred, and my proactive and vocal approach created a new opportunity for me.

The next challenge was to tackle fair lending compliance, and the role was offered to me. However, an outside consulting firm unfamiliar with the position and its role or significance to the continued growth and prosperity of the bank had undervalued the position in both title and compensation. Of course, I communicated this fact to my manager and raised my concerns. And my concerns were ignored. Drawing on the lived experiences in my youth from dealing with bullies and others who would attempt to take things from me, I came up with a strategy to win. My motivation was simple: $15,000 in additional income, a vice president title, stock options, a bonus, and more vacation time. It was all hanging in the balance, and I was determined to correct the consultant's lowball assessment for the position. I had my work cut out for me.

I was new to this area of banking and was told that I needed to prepare for and pass the federal regulator's fair lending compliance exam. I decided to incorporate it into the first part of my strategy: to be monumentally successful in my new role. That meant I had to obtain an excellent fair lending rating my first time out as the new fair lending manager. To do that, I created a fair lending program to train approximately 7,000 employees using modules that were appropriately based on each of their roles and their proximity to lending. I collaborated with colleagues in every area of the bank, created content, tests, monitoring rules, and results. I reported this to division and department leaders and ensured that all retail and client-facing employees completed the training modules.

The second part of my strategy was to be in the room to present the fair lending program to the regulators and senior management. This would later allow me to negotiate fair compensation and mitigate the possible claim of my inexperience in this new role. I anticipated that my manager would want to take full credit for my work, and I would not be allowed to participate in the compliance presentation. So, this strategy required street smarts. I put together a very comprehensive package to present. It included three five-inch binders. I worked on this for about six months with the assistance of many colleagues across all business units throughout our seven-state market area. It was voluminous, and I decided the best course of action was to work up to the day before the deadline and submit the three five-inch binders to my manager. It was too much information to digest, so this strategy ensured my seat at the table.

The morning before the exam, I gave my manager the binders to review and waited patiently for his response. Several hours later, he emerged from the doorway to my office. He praised the work that I did but, at the same time, realized there was no way he could digest that level of information overnight. Then, with reluctance on his face, he asked, "Are you free tomorrow? With the work you have done and the fact that you have been living with it for months, you are the best one to present this information." I checked my calendar, knowing full well that there was nothing on it. I was planning to be at that regulatory meeting. And I was well prepared to share the information I assembled.

The day came, all went well with the presentation, and the opening of the fair lending exam period was a success. Over the course of a couple of months, I responded to several inquiries while the examiners picked apart and reviewed the content of my exam package. The exam ended, and we waited for the results. Then we finally got word that we received an excellent fair lending exam rating.

Upon receiving that information, it was time to move forward to the next phase. Now was the moment to reexamine the dismissal of my request for additional compensation. Being new to the role no longer mattered as I had achieved results expected of a seasoned fair lending manager. I was certainly not a newbie. So, I brought forth my concerns, and after a few days with no response, I decided to escalate the matter to the director of human resources. I communicated to the HR director that I was not calling to cause any issues for my manager but to correct a situation that not only negatively impacted me but also other team members who were moving up the ladder and hitting that arbitrary maximum percentage pay increase. This was in addition to the consultant's errors in assessing the position.

I explained that, in my view, long-term employees would have to leave to reach their justified compensation level, and unfortunately, our replacements from outside would be brought in at the level that existing team members should be afforded. In my specific case, they would not be able to recruit my replacement with the compensation package I was provided. Fortunately, my message got through and my package was amended to my benefit. I was able to apply lessons from the streets to win in this corporate space. It was fighting corporate style with words, reasoning, and bottom-line logic instead of physical fighting, fear, intimidation, or threats.

Finally, there is the story of "*The Bully*." I have found that some people wear their ignorance like a badge of honor, and they are predisposed to assume their corporate title grants them privilege through positional power. As such, they believe they can rule over and dominate those who have lower-level titles. They are typically not prepared to deal with people who possess superior personal power. Personal power does not rely on positions or titles.

As I reflect on what prepared me for this, I must take a trip back to the neighborhood on a sizzling summer day. Over the years, I had amassed personal power that shielded me from any thoughts of inferiority, imposter syndrome, or any of the other issues and challenges that one could fall victim to in an environment where you are constantly having to fight microaggressions, twisted compliments, and putting people in check by telling them things like, "I don't like Polish jokes because they are told when there are no Polish people in the room. So, what kind of jokes do you tell when there are no Black people in the room?"

This is the benefit of positional power and establishing your own financial base. Your lifestyle is not dependent solely on your corporate job so you can speak up and do not ever need to compromise your values. And when people realize you are not intimidated or beholden to their paycheck and you just do not give a crap, you experience a profoundly liberating sense of freedom. This reality allowed me to be authentic throughout my career without fear. In some ways, it made the battles fun, and winning was rewarding!

Back to the story. There were about ten of us young boys waiting in line for the boys' club to open. Picture this: One of the neighborhood bullies walks up and decides to take a spot in front of the line. And the rule was that if you could not hold your spot and someone took it, you had to go to the back of the line. Dejected, a bit embarrassed, and too afraid to do anything about it, the boy in the front gave his spot to the bully and walked to the back of the line. I immediately started wondering why everyone was so afraid of this guy. I began to ponder: Can he even fight? I have never seen him fight. The more I thought about it, the angrier I became. Then the bully and I locked eyes. I started to think. There is about to be a fight, and it is going to be a knockdown, drag-out fight. It is going to take a couple of adults from inside the boys' club to pull us apart. Then I thought about what my dad used to say as I would leave the house, "Do not go out there starting any trouble, but if trouble finds you, I want you to make him feel right at home." I was about to put down the welcome mat for this bully. He just did not know it yet!

As our eyes locked, the bully began to walk towards me. He asked me what I was looking at. "You want to make something of it?" So, looking him right in the eyes with full authority, I said, "I am looking at nothing, and if I were in the front of the line, you would not be taking my spot." Of course, that angered him, so he decided it would be okay to show his dominance by shoving me. As he reached toward me, I punched him right in the nose! In that instant, I was expecting a mini–World War III. After all, this was the tough guy that everyone was afraid of. As he put one hand up to check his nose and saw blood, he said in a surprising whimper, "You made my nose bleed." I was incredibly surprised, a little disappointed, and a little relieved because fighting would typically get you sent home for the day, and I wanted to shoot pool in the game room. As the bully walked away, I told the boy who went to the back of the line that he could have his spot back.

Now let's fast forward to the corporate bully. He had not been with the company long and didn't work in our office daily, but he visited once a week or so to meet with members of his team. When he visited, he would say he wanted my office and that I could go work in one of the cubicles. So, in a colonizing fashion, he thought was just going to take my office. One of the lessons from the neighborhood, as you know by now, is that you should never let anyone take anything from you. To put this bully in his place, I certainly couldn't punch him in the nose to get him to back off. That would be grounds for immediate termination and assault charges. So, how should I manage this bullying type of aggression at work? I pondered that dilemma. Then, as I was about to leave the office one Saturday afternoon, it came to me. Since he does not want to play nice in the sandbox, I will dismantle the spare desk and relocate it to the mailroom. I thought this was a brilliant solution for the tough guy at the office. I went to work, taking the desk apart piece by piece and reassembling it in the mailroom. On Monday morning, the plan was all set even though I was not sure what day the bully would show up.

He didn't show up on Monday, and I was going to be out of the office for meetings the following day. So, I decided to do something I never had a reason to do before: lock my office and inform the team that if the bully shows up, they should let him know that no one has the key to my office. Sure enough, he showed up on the day I was out. I was told he peered through the window and saw that my desk had been moved to the center and the spare desk was gone. He was furious, and a showdown was imminent.

He came back in a day or two, and in true bully form, stormed into my office for the confrontation. He asked me where the spare desk was and who I thought I was. I told him I did not know what he was talking about. The calmer I was, the angrier and louder he became. "The spare desk—you moved it!" he said. "Yes," I said, "I moved it. It is in the mailroom. There is plenty of privacy back there."

Then, I stood up deliberately and added, "You know I work here, but I am not from here. You can lower your voice, or we can step outside." With that, he stormed out and called my manager, who was also a senior vice president. About fifteen minutes later, I got a call from my manager, who told me that this bully was a senior vice president and insinuated that working in a cubicle should be a consideration. I reminded him that he had used the spare desk, his boss had used the spare desk, and none of the other leaders who used the spare desk had ever been disrespectful or attempted to kick me out of my office. Furthermore, he was only in the area once every week or two, so he could use the spare desk in the mailroom or one of the cubicles. If the cubicles were good enough for me, then they should also be good enough for him. My manager replied that I needed to handle it, and my response was that I already had. The last word I had with the bully was to inform him that I would still be there when he was gone.

I left a few years later on my own terms. It took about a year to transition from my position as vice president and fair lending manager. After which, I spent about sixteen months as the Chief Administrative Officer for a public charter school. From there, I had the awesome opportunity to spend roughly five years golfing, camping, and traveling with my family, as well as spending quality time with my daughters during their formative years.

I've had a great professional journey in a world where some people occasionally treated me like I didn't belong, but those that mattered overwhelmingly respected me. The lessons learned and skills developed are used every day to benefit my community and my family. I have enjoyed representing my family, my people, and my community, and my journey has brought credibility from the streets to corporate suites. Therefore, I am filled with gratitude, peace, and no regrets.

**Phillip D. Woolfolk**

www.phillipwoolfolk.com

Phillip Woolfolk is not just a speaker; he's an author, coach, strategist, investor, and business builder with a mission to help high-achieving professionals and entrepreneurs break through financial ceilings, expand their business potential, and scale with sustainability.

As a speaker and coach Phillip delivers impactful presentations to audiences on: 1. The Journey Empowerment 2. Business Growth & Prosperity 3. Financial Empowerment & Wealth Building 4. Access to Capital and 5. Real Estate Investing. As an alternative lender, Phillip facilitates funding for real estate investors, builders, developers, and entrepreneurs.

# 7

# KETCH-A-FYAH!

## Dr. Sherone Smith-Sanchez

How can Black professionals accelerate and sustain high levels of success? We often face unique barriers and challenges in the workplace related to accepted behavior patterns and organizational culture connected to the dregs of colonialism. This toxicity can impede personal and professional advancement. We can, however, opt to accelerate and sustain positive momentum in our careers by cultivating certain attitudes and behaviors.

Motivational strategies that include developing passion, self-efficacy, resilience, and self-awareness can enable Black professionals to thrive. Those of us living in dark, toxic work cultures are the only ones capable of illuminating our own way by enacting these strategies. These truths are the result of more than 30 years where I have studied and practiced leadership in both the secular and clergy realms.

Hence, these important realizations concerning the need for a system for personal motivation evolved over time and are in part outcomes of my Jamaican upbringing. Jamaican proverbs I heard as a child moved from being the sayings of wise elders to becoming words I held onto for comfort and guidance while moving up the career ladder as a Black immigrant woman in the United States.

Thus, I have come to embrace the theme of fire which was one of my Grand-Aunt Ada's favorites in her recited proverbs. Her phrase 'Ketch-a-fyah' became analogous with igniting passionate, personal, and professional advancement. Similarly, Grandma Muriel would say, "Empty coal pot cyah ketch fyah", (an empty coal pot can't catch fire) and that emphasized for me the importance of being full of the necessary self-awareness, faith, education, and resiliency to sustain the ignited fire's momentum. Concurrently, these proverbs were later emphasized and formalized as I learned the theories (to be discussed later) that aligned with them moving through the halls of formal education.

My formal education started at the Jamaica School of Art. This was a vibrant artistic mecca for fine and performing artists from around the world. There, I was encouraged to celebrate our diversity while being proud of who I was as a Black Lioness. Later, I transferred to a world-renowned art school in New York. I gained real insight there into the Black workforce's world in America. The need for social justice awareness for this community was elicited by a rude awakening one fateful night.

On this night, as I tearfully worked alone in the studio at my new school, doubting my own abilities for the first time ever, I heard, "Oh, so you are the new token!" I looked up to find the young Black woman who graduated the semester prior to my arrival. While her remark was sarcasm, she confirmed that the constant denigration I was experiencing from white students and professors was not in my mind. She also verified my suspicion that I was the only Black student in the undergraduate fine arts department. This brave angel recommended I join the Black Students Association to relieve my sense of isolation. There, I met the other Black representatives of each department and confirmed that in the 1980s, the Black student was not to be celebrated by this school. We were expected to be quiet and grateful while enduring the insults of professors daily. It was apparent that the all-white faculty's attitude was one of mere tolerance of students who only filled a quota, with no incentive to inspire our success.

The persecution was so intense that I woke up every morning with a sickening feeling of dread, expecting to be verbally assaulted at school. Professors frequently said cruel things in class that were thinly veiled microaggressions. One man who taught every required course in the department was open with his evil comments and said things to me during class discussions like, "Sherone, shut your f\*\*king mouth!" In response, I worked twice as hard as all others, leaving home at 5 a.m. to get to the studio before working two jobs in between classes and leaving the studio at 10 or 11 pm for my hour and a half commute home. It was during my first year in an American university, experiencing this profound mental anguish that I first realized the crucial need for systemic change regarding how Black professionals were schooled and viewed.

## RESILIENCE

As is the case for many of us, failure was not an option in my American college experience; resilience was. Black professionals must cultivate resilience, which is defined as the ability to recover from setbacks, adapt to change, and keep going in the face of adversity. [1] Without resiliency, the Black professional's work experience can become discouraging due to discrimination, microaggressions, glass ceilings, unfair policies, and other forms of systemic and interpersonal racism. However, leaning into emotional and mental resilience allows us to bounce back from failures and continue progressing despite the mobbing. Resilience is a muscle that must be strengthened over time through small challenges. [2]

At the start of my American schooling experience, my uncle, who endured similar problems as a Black graduate student at another American university in the 70's, kept telling me that I had as much right to be there as everyone else. He was correct.

---

[1] King, George A., and Cathrine Rothstein. "Resilience." Oxford Research Encyclopedia of Psychology (2016).
[2] Jackson, La Tanya, PhD. "7 ways for Black professionals to establish resilience and thrive at work." Forbes, June 19, 2020.
https://www.forbes.com/sites/latanyajackson/2020/06/19/7-ways-for-black-professionals-to-establish-resilience-and-thrive-at-work.

When faced with this type of work and school oppression, we should all believe him and all the elders who have gone before. We should refuse to quit. This is an example of how culture and the support of our elders and ancestors can push us forward. Here, I lived another proverb I learned as a Jamaican child: "Forward ever. Backward. NEVER!" I received my BFA degree, too exhausted to even attend my graduation. Thirty years later, after attaining three more degrees with similar experiences, to my pleasant surprise, I was invited to walk in the centennial graduation ceremony for my undergrad alma mater. I wept the entire day and was thankful that someone in that university gave some semblance of the long-awaited justice that we four Black alumni representing four decades deserved.

The complexity of this issue may be seen in the fact that back then, even though the insults directed at me were obvious, most white students ignored them. At first, some tried helping me, but then they were targeted too. Having lived this experience and risen in a leadership career where I have often been among a few Black professionals at the proverbial top, I have learned the crucial need for allyship where the ally displays a deep sense of social justice and bravery. That experience and many current professional experiences show that people often ignore racism even when it is extreme and direct. While overt racism is usually ignored in professional and higher education settings, even well-intentioned allies who try to support Black colleagues can face backlash. Though standing up against injustice is morally right, many refrain from helping victims due to fear of also being targeted. Nelson, et al. concur that social repercussions for confronting discrimination frequently deter witnesses from intervening, allowing racism to proliferate unchecked.[1]

The risks faced by allies demonstrate the deep systemic forces that maintain racial barriers and prevent true equality in the

---

[1] Nelson, Jessica C. et al. "Why Are Some Allies Effective While Others Are Not? A Teory of Ally Effectiveness." Perspectives on Psychological Science 16, no. 6 (November 2021): 1278-1296.

workplace. Still, allyship remains vital to disrupting oppression, even if allies sometimes sacrifice their own comfort or status through their solidarity. [1] The complexity of the Black professional's need for systemic motivational strategy and allyship lies in the fact that these organizational behaviors are ingrained in accepted policies and practices, developed in a colonialism and post-colonialism atmosphere. Most workforce development policies in the United States were designed to maintain the status of the male, white professional. Without the confirmation and affirmation of colleagues that this is in fact the case, a Black Professional can be lulled into believing that they are mistaken. Thus, most organizations have normalized negative behaviors, and like my allies at school, have employees who learned that support of the Black professional/fellow student can be detrimental to their own advancement.

## PASSION

It is imperative that all understand that this is not a Black person issue; rather, it is a societal issue. So, a deep understanding of the phenomena of the Black workforce experience is necessary for humankind's forward movement. Most importantly, for the Black professional to achieve success as part of any workforce we must understand and transcend the effects of our colonial past by starting with our inner fire, or passion for advancing our area of expertise in society. Passion is defined as "a strong inclination toward an activity that people like, that they find important, and in which they invest time and energy." [2] Having passion for one's work and career can be a significant driver of success for Black professionals. When people are passionate about their job, they are intrinsically motivated to put in long hours, constantly improve,

---

[1] Brown, Kathleen, and Elizabeth Vida June. "Retaliation Against Those Who Support the Cause." Journal of the Society for Organizational Learning 2 (2000).

[2] Vallerand, Robert J. "On passion for life activities: The dualistic model of passion." Advances in experimental social psychology 49 (2015): 97-193.

take on challenges, and go above and beyond.[1] This passion often leads to superior performance and achievements which destroy the colonial myth of white male dominance. Most importantly, passion makes work enjoyable rather than just a paycheck, which reduces burnout. By cultivating passion for their careers, we can accelerate our professional success. As explained earlier, my Grand-Aunt Ada's phrase 'Ketch-a-fyah' corresponds with igniting passionate, personal, and professional advancement in my life. This fiery passion served me well as I worked for my city as a Civil Servant. The story that demonstrates this begins with my experience on a Monday in July of 2006.

*** 

One quiet Monday morning, I walked out of a cold elevator and stepped into the harsh, even icier atmosphere of my civil service department. I had arrived to assume my new leadership role. My new team's icicle eyes glared, stabbing me like multiple dagger-like shards. They had clearly congregated by the elevator awaiting my arrival but said nothing as they pointedly turned their backs in rehearsed protest at my promotion. These were my colleagues, my Black SISTAHS with whom I had enjoyed years of work! I had hoped they would be happy for me. After all, they had watched me power through to do my best work as a professional, struggling to get these four degrees while caring for a husband who had a stroke at 26 and our 5 children. They knew that I was a union member and a team player from the trenches, just like them. They knew I respected them, and was more than ready to discuss and affect new, cutting-edge changes with them... Didn't they? No, for multiple social, cultural, and organizational psychological reasons, they did not.

---

[1] Perrewé, Pamela L., Halbesleben, Jonathon RB and Mayfield, Jacqueline. "A motivation-based model of work–family conflict." Journal of Organizational Behavior: The International Journal of Industrial, Occupational and Organizational Psychology and Behavior 28, no. 2 (2007): 145-160.

This was the anticlimactic end to a saga where months prior, I learned that my promotion to a departmental leadership role was officially postponed. The delay lasted six months while coworkers, dear to my heart, formally filed a union grievance protesting my promotion. My stunned soul screamed, "WHAT??" They insisted that my hard-earned qualifications and experience were irrelevant in comparison to the expected traditional system of social promotion.

My 'rival' had been a civil servant for more than 30 years, and understandably, from her perspective, she had earned the position because she "put in the time." She was so upset that I was invited to apply that upper management had the security team escort her out. I respected this colleague for her sheer endurance and phenomenal levels of knowledge about the history of systems in local government. She had endured decades of debasement that occurred as a Black civil servant and kowtowed to more upper management than anyone else there. It was her turn to literally leave the field and be rewarded with golden years in the big house.

This analogy is deliberate because, as we've established, remaining professional systems are still blatantly reflective of much of the African Diaspora's enslaved and colonized past. In the United States, we still live the trajectories, which were clearly designed for us, crafted to maintain systems in the tokenism game. It is the same game where I was an unwilling contestant in college. It happened again years later in professional workspaces. I believe this obscure game is meant to keep us trudging on wheels that give the illusion of movement as we maintain society's key infrastructures with little reward. The success of the modern colonialism game in all aspects of American society (religious as well as secular circles) is dependent upon the mindless mental enslavement enveloping us from childhood.

Our ancestors had to play this game often to live, and even then, many died trying. Those martyrs died so that we do not have to keep playing it. There are now other ways to advance in a manner that is meaningful and key to the advancement of our children and society in general. Unit workers and middle management in my city's governmental system were predominantly people of color, while those at the very top were mostly Caucasians, with a sprinkling of color to give the illusion of equality. This illusion comprised the general design of a game meant to pit groups against each other as we vied for the few leadership spots we were allowed.

As the months of protest dragged on, I waited patiently and endured well-meaning colleagues who told me I was "playing a dangerous game by accepting this position." as well as strange staff meetings where terroristic oppressive tricks and tormenting tactics were used by these same colleagues to belittle my every move. They told me that I needed to put in my time and wait my turn to enter the 'Big House.' Waiting my turn meant that I would play the groveling part of the game and wait to become the one "lucky" enough to finally make it in. Promotion based upon tokenism is just as harmful as no promotion at all. It assumes that the person in the leadership seat was not qualified enough to make it. Promotion to the big house with the big job based upon arbitrary rules means that one who occupies that space is subject to the rule-makers and not meant to be a thinker or innovator. What do you do when that opportunity to move into leadership arises? As I have learned, getting through the front door might be uncomfortable. It might even be the result of the wheels of tokenism, but it is what we do when we occupy the space that matters.

I had no intention of going to the big government 'house' to maintain the systems of oppression or the status quo that had existed for centuries. My plan was to peacefully invite others to help me to dismantle this iniquitous house. Brick by brick, we would deconstruct systems, examine them, and decide if, in our new paradigm, those pieces fit after all. We would embrace the shifts that disruption can bring that lead to pioneering practice. To this day, I sign every email, "In Umoja" to teach and embrace lessons of unity.

So, on this, my first day entering civil service leadership, as I walked into my purpose, I felt leadership lioness energy taking over. My help, as they say, came from the Lord. As I looked in a mix of fleeting sadness and wry amusement, I smiled at my colleagues, most unaware that they were perpetuating colonial narratives. Each turned their backs one by one in solidarity to avoid greeting me directly on my first day as their leader. I smiled because they exhibited the strength of our ancestors, and I knew that strength could be supported and celebrated in our future work.

I chose to defrost the air with unity, love, and respect, greeting them with, "Good morning! I'll see you at 10 for our meeting!" I was on fire, and no amount of ice was going to dissolve my passion! This passion was about shifting a system that had been in stasis for 75 years since its inception. I had published the research for my dissertation and proved that the casualties of the public service system I was asked to help lead were my own impoverished Black and brown village youth.[1] As brothers and sisters in the struggle to create meaningful systemic change for our children, we had no time for petty squabbles.

You see, beloved, those of us in the trenches know that infighting is only a result of communal sadness and disappointment. So, my simple strategy was to consistently convey respect for their collective knowledge and experience as we worked to build a shared vision. The shortened end of this story is, once this team understood my intention to create a safe, passionate, research-focused department, they became the joy of my career. Fear had rendered them and the department frozen, but the fire that defrosted us was personal and professional passion.

In more than thirty years as a Black lioness in leadership, I have negotiated these microaggressions in all aspects of my world, both as a secular and church leader. So, I can attest to the fact that

---

[1] Sherone Andrienne Smith-Sanchez, "The Alternative Care Experiences of Those Who Wait on NYC Subsidized Childcare Waiting Lists" (Ed.D dissertation, Columbia University, 2003).

Black women in leadership choose this high road every day. We survive by faith in our God, grit, and grace. I had grown used to transcending this battle and had not come to wage a war with my sisters and brothers. Instead, I had come to exchange ideas, be taught, and teach them. As Black women who are born to leadership, we can unwisely choose to partake of cocktails of unnecessary, energy-draining, catty competitiveness, mixed with the dregs of colonialism and misogyny, or we can light up the room with lioness energy!

By now beloved, you have learned two things: I am a storyteller, and whenever this story mentions fire, it is a euphemism for focused passion. This kind of passion is zeal that is accompanied by work that changes the world. Most importantly, a focused fire will change you! Focused fire energy transcends the depths and doldrums of life's gutters, whether they are personal or professional. So... how do we get IT? How do we attain that fire that lights our stairway to innovation and helps us to function on a conscious plane whether we are in the house, the field, or a sterile office? Simply put... You gotta catch fire before you can burn!

### You Gotta Catch Fire Before You Can Burn!

To develop focused fire, it must be ignited by something. I learned the ways of my ancestors well, and every Sunday, while I lived on the island, my parents patiently taught me to "Ketch up di fyah" (light the fire) by using wood chips and paper to help in the igniting process. Similarly, to circumvent systems of oppression, we must be ignited with the spark of our why. So... What's your why? To burn with focused, useful fire that results in personal and professional elevation as well as innovation, we must first define our WHY. Are you pursuing leadership as a career or lifestyle because someone else said, "This is the way"? Or is your narrative, "I am pursuing this career because I am called to it, and I am good at it"? What is your WHY?

As a clear example to those who will come after us, and for the sake of our own well-being, we need to define our reasons for pursuing our goals. Those reasons help to craft the responses to issues that arise at work and in our daily lives. In the story of my first day as a civil service supervisor, my 'why' was steeped in my goals for my village. The civil service arena, like many microcosms of society, is really evidence of the dregs of colonialism, where we in the African Diaspora have been socialized to compete. Institutionalized racism is built on the premise that if we are encouraged to backbite, sell each other out, and vie for fabricated notions of power, we will be unable to rise in society as the true leaders we are. This was evidenced in my city's civil service system, where the thousands of very able workers (mostly people of color) were led by middle managers who squabbled amongst themselves often to maintain a status where they were made content to push paper and not be among the top leaders who were mostly Caucasians.

Now this does not mean that there is a little room where white people are sitting around gleefully rubbing their hands as they concoct ways to force Black and Latino staff to fight a bloody duel under the glaring fluorescent lights. Instead, we are all traveling on a journey of unconscious biases set in motion by more than 400 years of oppression, marinating in our DNA, and thus developed from childhood. Consequently, many of my Caucasian coworkers often lived the inherited life of entitlement to which they were born. Some were willing to be allies and help to forge a new future for us by dismantling the system but were unsure as to how to do that without becoming societal pariahs.

The only one who can light the way is the one who has forged a path in the dark—us, the Black professionals. We have a responsibility to refuse to be marginalized and push past institutional racism with the fortitude of one who has purpose by refusing to fight useless minimal battles within our village. If I fight my village aimlessly, then I hurt my village pointlessly. So, our primary point is: *You gotta catch fire before you can BURN* with passion, promise and purpose. Catching fire means laser-like focus on why you are moving forward and envisioning yourself as a daughter or son of the Most High. It means you have the vision of the emperor or empress you were born to be; you understand that you are both successful and worthy of success; you are the head and not the tail, the victor and NOT the victim, the called, beloved and NOT the coward. Believing in yourself and in your God's ability to help you to your next level.

**Dr. Sherone Smith-Sanchez**
https://talawahturf.com
As founder of consulting firm Talawah Turf International (TTI), Dr. Sherone Smith-Sanchez partners with religious and secular leaders to build individual and team capacity for data-driven community service and engagement. TTI provides grant writing, professional development, technical assistance, and coaching focused on developing efficient, evidence-based organizations.

# 8

# A SEAT AT THE TABLE, NO VOICE IN THE ROOM

## Dr. Mary Darden-Robinson

That was it…. As I pulled up, once more, to a prospective new work environment, I took it all in. It was a sunny day in this affluent community, and on a large, green, manicured lot stood a beautiful two-story brick building with flowers and beautiful landscaping circling the building. I thought to myself, "I can see myself here taking my daily break under one of the tall trees to read or eat lunch in between business meetings." Off in the distance, construction crews were busy expanding the facility. I took a deep breath, then exhaled as I switched to my heels, grabbed my portfolio, and headed into my interview.

I shook the hand of my interviewer and shared my name; I waited to see if she would acknowledge our prior meetings, as I had, on more than one occasion, attended training that she either sat on the board for or facilitated prior. But as I had come to experience with countless other professionals, she didn't appear to make any mention of our prior meetings. Nonetheless, we continued into the interview space, and I shared my educational background and experience. I even added a discussion that I was eclectic and used creativity to evaluate, assess, and manage mental health and substance use programs in the past. The discussion went well, and I was advised that I was the candidate that would be able to take the program to the next level. I felt as though I was about to begin my next exciting adventure. As the interview concluded, the interviewer alluded to being somewhat familiar with my name, and it was at that moment that I decided to share our prior meetings. I left the experience excited about what was to come.

Within a few days, I signed my offer letter and then gave notice to my employer. Shortly thereafter came a call I would never have been ready for. I answered the phone; the interviewer on the other side explained that the agency decided not to move forward with me in the position. I could not believe what I was hearing. Although empathetic, the message was clear and unchanging. I thought to myself, "That is it!" What she didn't know is that remaining at my present place of employment was not an option, although she loosely appeared to use this option to soften the blow of her message. I was essentially being forced into unemployment. I was further advised that there were not any alternative positions at that facility that would meet my employment needs at that time. In a state of shock, I asked about any similar opportunities at other locations managed by the interviewer that could meet my needs to avoid being forced into unemployment. And in came the bait-and-switch setup.

## THE BAIT AND SWITCH...

Even though I was disappointed with the experience, unemployment was not an option. The role appeared on paper as being an executive leadership type of position and somewhat equivalent to the role that I previously accepted; however, upon beginning my employment at the other facility, it became clear that the positions were very different. The clientele and expectations were different. I would not be responsible for leading and spearheading a program as a director. Instead, and with the same title, I would now be responsible for direct care services and have less of a leadership role. Moreover, the clientele that I would be responsible for would no longer be professionals such as attorneys, doctors, and nurses. Instead, I would be working with the underserved population. I could not help but think there was more to the story than what was shared with me. Several weeks after I started with the other site, someone who looked nothing like me was promoted into a role just like the role I initially accepted.

Essentially, this experience felt like a demotion and was emotionally taxing. I had to show up every day, authentically, while working through an internal battle. So, I laced up my boots and decided once more that this would not be a workspace that would be safe for me. It was clear at this point that I could not trust my employer, and without trust, I knew longevity would not be possible.

Researchers and scholars alike have most recently begun to explore the correlation between cultural diversity and psychological safety within the workplace. Agbanobi and Asmelash define psychological safety as "the belief that everyone can pitch risky ideas and challenge the status quo without retaliation or judgment."[11] Nonetheless, psychological safety is not absolute. As a Black woman in the workplace, using my voice to challenge directions is seen as insubordinate. I am berated and then belittled by leadership.

For this chapter, the concept of safety will be assessed through the lens of the mental health and substance use field as it relates to the educated Black woman striving to advance into executive and corporate leadership. It is important to consider that as an individual with two strikes, being a female and a member of a minority group, transitioning into executive and corporate

---

1 Agbanobi, Agatha. "Creating Psychological Safety for Black Women at Your Company." Harvard Business Review, May 22, 2023.
https://hbr.org/2023/05/creating-psychological-safety-for-black-women-at-your-company.

leadership within the mental health and substance use fields can feel almost impossible.

## THE PLACE HOLDER

As a Black woman navigating the mental health and substance use industry, I have become astute to the concept of *The Place Holder.* As I sat anxiously, I awaited what I knew would be the third failed discussion regarding my pay reconsideration request, my heart began to rapidly beat, my palms were sweaty, and my voice somewhat quivered. I waited for the outcome report from my supervisor and the director of programs. She said, "It doesn't appear as if you are doing anything beyond what your role requires, so there is not any departmental support for a pay increase." What I heard was, we *don't value you, and now that you are speaking up, we are going to beat you into submission.* Figuratively, of course.

How could she make such an assessment? I was responsible for assessing the overall impact of the program in addition to creating workflows, guidance documents, executive summaries, policy development, and business plans. Those tasks belonged to the two of them, not me! Her comments were so inaccurate, demeaning, and disrespectful. After all, the message that was being delivered by leadership was that I had not accomplished the goals required of me, especially as a minority, to even get a chance to figuratively "sit at the table."

Time after time, I asked to see an example of such documents that my predecessor would have completed, and I was quickly silenced with "She left before creating these documents" or some other comment that suggested that she was incapable of creating the items requested. I thought to myself, "Yeah, I bet she did leave before completing the tasks, which I'm sure they would've hijacked." Who would want to freely hand over their work when they knew they would be totally erased from the script? Not I.

I was being used as a pawn. I finally realized it after I noticed a specific pattern. When I offered any rebuttal or asked questions, my supervisor would discard my feedback like random chatter that did not deserve a place in the discussion. Shortly after this unproductive meeting, I went online and frivolously began to apply for new roles. I was willing to start all over again rather than to allow the gaslighting chess moves! During this process, I found that I was constantly called and invited to interview time and time again; however, I wasn't securing the roles. So, I simply decided that if the organization I was interviewing with did not want me, then I did not want them.

I refer to this experience as *The Place Holder Phenomenon*. You see, I was simply the candidate who was offered the interview; unbeknownst to myself, I would never truly be considered for the position. I simply was offered the interview so the organization could legally hire the individual they had already been courting for some time. I did not realize that it was in fact a placebo role which was already figuratively filled. Some refer to this as "the old next in line." And it happened again and again. It happened so much that I created my own blacklist of organizations I would no longer interview with.

In 2021 the APA published a public apology "to communities of color for perpetuating systemic racism."[1] As the largest professional psychology organization, while I can appreciate admitting to taking a part in fueling the systemic racism vehicle, I am empowered to continue to challenge organizations to do more. It takes all of us to use our voice and advocate for change, as well as uncover and highlight behaviors that serve to continue that racism. Sitting on the sidelines quietly and looking the other way is not an option. To better understand the experience of a woman of color striving to reach executive and corporate leadership, it is imperative to provide an account of some of the barriers she faces.

---

[1]"Apology to people of color for APA's role in promoting, perpetuating, and failing to challenge racism, racial discrimination, and human hierarchy in U.S." 2021. American Psychological Association. https://www.apa.org/about/policy/racism-apology.

## The Diversity-Desert Workplace

For as long as I can remember, formal education has been valued within my immediate family. *Get your education, and no one can take that away from you!* This was a mantra repeated time after time by my mother, and I believed and bought into this idea of using my education to catapult me into rooms and discussions that were difficult to infiltrate otherwise. It was my hope that my education would push me from providing direct service to becoming a senior and/or an executive member of corporate leadership within my field of study.

So, I defied the odds by obtaining a doctorate in psychology. Or did I really? With the title of *Doctor* and several certificates and licenses in tow, I thought I was ready to rise beyond the arbitrary glass ceiling. To truly appreciate this task, I recall being counted out as it relates to obtaining one license and any education beyond high school, certainly not a doctorate. Regardless of my hard work and diligence, I continued to find myself day after day in a diversity-desert workspace. Having a solid foundation and shared definition for such a workspace is essential to fully understanding the experience of being on the receiving end of unfair treatment within a diversity-desert workspace.

It may seem at first glance that a workplace is not a diversity desert, but it is important to consider not only the employer's verbal messaging but also their nonverbal cues and behaviors. An employer may verbalize that their agency is inclusive and values diversity, all the while using empty catchphrases and slogans, promoting inequity, marginalization, bullying, microaggressions, and honoring the glass ceiling.

### Barrier One: Acceptance

I have openly joked with those close to me that I wish I could participate in interviews while the panel sits with their backs to me, much like the show *The Voice*. My mother always said that there is some truth in jokes that we make. Through the twenty-plus years that I have worked within the field, acceptance has been a goal never to be accomplished. Acceptance in its true form to me consists of knowing that my voice within the workspace is seen as respected and valued. It has been my experience that in meetings whenever I share a contrary opinion or experience, I am met with resistance and immediately cut off. I have become keen to look for the other shoe to drop, which usually comes to the forefront as retaliatory behaviors. Some examples experienced consist of having prior approved training canceled, being uninvited to meetings, and being micromanaged on projects. I can also recall sharing regulations and guidelines mandated within the mental health and substance use fields to support program evaluation and being told, "I totally disagree; I am sure that's not a regulation," and questioned with, "Could you tell me which regulation that is?" to embarrass me in the presence of others. Regardless of my extensive experience within the field, I was immediately spoken to in a manner that was demeaning, unsupported, and publicly shaming.

Acceptance goes hand in hand with the prior-mentioned psychological safety. Organizations could benefit from prioritizing these two values. Research has indicated that without them, individuals are exiting the field in vast numbers. Although I was familiar with the lack of acceptance within the workspace due to my ethnicity, being judged and treated unfairly by those who look like me was unfamiliar early in my career. I had no idea that I was about to preview what my leadership journey would look like through this same lens. It did not take long for me to be challenged to make a choice regarding my authenticity in the workplace. My professional growth, as a young, eclectic professional, came at a price. When I decided to remain authentic and faithful to myself, I realized the cost would be high. Then it finally happened: I was selected for a middle management role. In addition to being predominantly African American, the agency I would be joining also served as a training ground for leadership with one caveat: this employer belonged to a community in which you had to be accepted.

The highest-ranking person in the agency assessed me from head to toe as part of my initial introduction to the Executive Leadership Team. I felt a sense of disappointment, which was obvious. I was immediately put on notice that the leadership at this agency did not like colored hair and/or creative nails. Having this experience came from a place of unfamiliarity, once again, from those who look like me—which challenged my prior experience. Nonetheless, I was shown contempt because I thrived.

**Barrier Two: The Mascot**

I tend to believe that my sheer presence as an African American female with red sister locks and colorfully painted and artistically designed nails has been used to paint the portrait of a diversity-friendly and aligned workspace. That couldn't be further from the truth! You see, my qualifications were always an afterthought. Even though I was typically hired into leadership roles, the glass ceiling was always right there, ever present, hitting me on the shoulder as a reminder that to have any voice in this discussion, I had to present in an outdated ideal of professionalism as defined by the organization, which typically did not align with my eclectic and creative style. By choosing my authenticity over the agency's antiquated ideals surrounding professionalism, I would have to intervene, insert, and challenge the status quo in the professional environment. Even though I knew doing so would set me up to be misunderstood, misinterpreted, targeted, bullied, and made to be an outcast, I chose my own self-worth. It is unfortunate that as a Black woman, feelings of uncertainty speak to the idea that in choosing myself and showing up authentically as myself, I will most likely be limiting my opportunities and any upward mobility.

A word of advice: If you find yourself in such a situation, it is imperative to consider that you are not made to fit in!

*You are not made to be everyone's cup of tea, but you are an acquired taste!*

—Unknown

This quote helps me to stay grounded while honoring myself. In addition, it assists me with returning to homeostasis in times of difficulty, especially whenever I have found myself in a diverse desert workspace.

**Barrier Three: Hijacking and Ghostwriting**

As an employer, do not support hijacking and ghostwriting activities! "Can you give that to me in a Word document?" was always predictably commonplace. Being given directives such as preparing a written summary upon completion of the event to be sent to a reviewer and executive leadership, along with city leadership for reporting, were also all too familiar instructions throughout my career. Rather than having my name attached to the documents or being provided any opportunity to be acknowledged for the research, time, and effort I put into numerous edits I completed, my name was constantly removed in favor of a member of the leadership team.

As a leader, one of your responsibilities is to prepare your employees to be ready to enter rooms where their names are being mentioned and for them to be able to authentically grow beyond their role. For example, I can recall being responsible for contributing to a state-funded and review document. Upon being asked about being mentioned as responsible for parts of the document, I was told that my name would not be noted, as this document always listed the names of members of the executive leadership team. Although, at first glance, this may have seemed feasible, I was aware that the addition of my name was appropriate based on my experience with the same document. My request was not considered or honored, and I felt a sense of dismissal. Here is a little something to think about: being a ghostwriter can be a profitable, exciting, and creative experience. However, I encourage leadership to consider how this role may impact a teammate, especially when there is a power and role differential. Such behavior can leave an employee feeling like the victim of creative hijacking.

As a professionally trained therapist by trade, I challenge workspaces, especially diversity-desert workspaces, to consider the importance of promoting trauma-informed workspaces. This idea of trauma-informed workspaces suggests that, just as we would with a client, it is imperative to assume that anyone that we encounter could have experienced some level of inequity within their employment history.

### Dr. Mary Darden-Robinson
Leveraging 20+ years as a private sector therapist, Dr. Mary Darden-Robinson emphasizes overall wellness and resilience for Hampton Roads adolescents and families across community settings, lending her expertise in program assessment, evaluation, and strategic planning to guide behavioral health organizations. Her eclectic style is grounded in CBT and MI.

# 9

# THE CALL IS COMING FROM INSIDE THE HOUSE

## Public Service Workers Are Ready to Serve, Rarely Respected

NICOLE D. VICK

"If you're not at the table, you're on the menu," my professor declared. I was in one of my favorite undergrad public policy classes in the late 1990s. I looked around to see if anyone else knew what my professor was talking about. Seeing no glimmer of familiarity or understanding in anyone's eyes, I returned my focus to the lecture.

My professor was a Black woman at the large PWI (predominantly white institution) I attended, which was one of the reasons I loved her class. In a space where not many people looked like me, she was there as an inspiration and a glimmer of hope. As she continued the lecture, she explained that marginalized populations had to make sure they were at decision-making tables so that their communities were not "on the menu," displaced, underfunded, demoralized, ignored, disrespected, etc. It made sense to me at the time.

More than 20 years later, I've shared with my former professor (who is now a friend and colleague) that I'm not so sure about her words. I've since learned that "we" are always on the menu, whether we are at the table or not, and that the effort to get to the table, stay there, and be effective in ensuring our communities get what they need can be an exercise in futility. Even worse, we pay the greatest cost—our physical and mental health.

I first learned that the world was different for people who looked like me in the 8th grade. In 1991, the Rodney King beating, the murder of Latasha Harlins, and the ensuing civil unrest taught me very important and difficult lessons about the value of Black lives. It was incredibly devastating and very scary to watch the businesses that my family frequented be vandalized and destroyed. These incidents, and a few others, taught me that the criminal justice system was designed to harm Black people. As I got older and entered the workforce, I came to understand that every system in society devalues Black lives in much the same way. I believe those experiences, along with a family history of public service, steered me towards a career in public health.

While trying to finish my undergraduate degree, I took a job as a student worker at the local health department in my town. One of my responsibilities was to answer a hotline where people could get information, resources, and treatment for sexually transmitted infections. Those times were quite interesting. There was the one guy that would call every week like clockwork and request dozens of free condoms mailed to him, which we gladly sent. There was another guy that would call regularly to ask for help in putting on a condom, and at some point, he'd say, "Yeah, I'm trying to put one on now, and I'm having a hard time," much to the shock of whoever answered his call. Most of our calls were from people who were scared or worried and needed help finding healthcare or medication, and I was happy to be able to help. At the time, I was also the young mother of a 3-year-old daughter born prematurely during my second semester of college. It was quite ironic to be a statistic (a teen mother of a preterm baby) while trying to forge a path that would ensure my family's future economic stability. Although I was just learning about public health at the time, the impact of the systems that perpetuate poor health had already impacted my life in many ways. I bore witness to:

**Lack of access to healthy food in my South Los Angeles neighborhood.** I currently live half a mile away from a national grocery store that closed in May 2021, allegedly because the parent company of the grocery chain did not want to pay their employees, who were mostly Black and brown, an additional $5 in COVID-related hero pay mandated by the City of Los Angeles in March 2021.[1] To date, there is no replacement grocery store in the area.

**Violence hovered over my community and trauma surfaced afterwards.** I came of age in South Los Angeles during the 1980s and 1990s and witnessed heightened gang violence as well as the civil unrest that occurred in my community in 1992 that still impacts the community currently.

**Lack of jobs and economic growth crippled the area.** Since the end of World War II, Black people in Los Angeles have faced challenges in finding work due to discriminatory policies and practices, changes in business practices that closed large factories and plants, and a shift towards lower-wage non-union jobs that left many underemployed or unemployed. In South Los Angeles, Blacks were shut out of lucrative careers in the automotive and aerospace industries and steered towards factory and other low-wage jobs that soon left the community due to globalization.[2]

Black women in public health have a double consciousness. I liken it to holding both the benefit and the burden of the work at the same time. I have the benefit of my education

---

[1] Slauson Girl, "Community Reacts to Kroger Closing Ralphs on Crenshaw and Slauson." Slauson Girl | Los Angeles News From A South Central Native, October 10, 2022. https://slausongirl.com/community-reacts-to-kroger-closing-ralphs-on-crenshaw-and-slauson/.

[2] Reft, Ryan. "Los Angeles Black Worker Center Pushes for Inclusion", Tropics of Meta - Historiography for the Masses, April 4, 2016. https://tropicsofmeta.com/2016/04/04/los-angeles-black-worker-center-pushes-for-inclusion/

and work experience to be able to understand the root causes of some of the most pervasive public health issues of our time, but I also hold the burden of understanding the impact of institutional racism on the health of the Black community in a deeply personal and intimate way. I imagine that Black women in social work, child protective services, and other social services agencies experience this as well. Black folks experience double consciousness in a variety of settings, including the workplace.

W.E.B. DuBois coined the term "double consciousness" to explain the tension that Black Americans hold between their Blackness and their Americanness in various settings.[1] The main point of DuBois's thoughts on double consciousness is that the existence of the color line prevents "the full recognition of humanity by racialized groups." Bell documents this biculturalism as inherent in Black professional life and how both race and racism inform and impact the psyche of Black people at work generally and Black women specifically.

I had my own experience with double consciousness in the workplace that shook me. Several years ago, I was asked to attend a training on structural and institutional racism along with a hundred or so coworkers and a few community partners that were invited. These types of trainings were gaining traction in public health because of the focus on health equity and the social determinants of health.

On the day of the training, I made my way into the brightly lit auditorium. I saw a colleague from a local HIV/AIDS health care organization who is also a good friend and took a seat next to him. The presentation began with a slide deck displayed on a large screen. At some point, a slide appeared that showed the many ways that the Black community is disproportionately negatively impacted by every single system in American society. From education to employment, we were behind. There was a second

---

[1] Itzigsohn, José, and Karida Brown. "SOCIOLOGY AND THE THEORY OF DOUBLE CONSCIOUSNESS: W. E. B. Du Bois's Phenomenology of Racialized Subjectivity." *Du Bois review* 12, no. 2 (2015): 231–248.

slide that showed the disproportionate benefit white people experienced from these systems.

I looked over at my friend, and we gave each other the Black people's "this is some BS" look. I muttered expletives under my breath, unable to hold back my feelings, even though the executive managers were just one row ahead of me. I don't think I've ever felt anger and sadness in a work setting before. It wasn't pretty. I struggled to remain professional in a space where my people's struggles were displayed for all to see. In that space, I felt both the benefit of understanding why my people suffer and the burden of suffering in the same space. To be fair, this was not new information to me, but the way it was shown "hit different." I walked away from that training feeling hopeless.

Afterwards, several of my female coworkers and I discussed via email how disillusioned the training left us feeling and lamented the lack of support for our well-being. I didn't realize it at the time, but my psychological safety was being compromised. Psychological safety as a concept has its foundation in organizational change. Schein and Bennis theorized that psychological safety was important in ensuring individuals felt secure and capable of taking chances.[1] It is defined as "one's perception of consequences for taking interpersonal risk in their work environment"[2] and making decisions to proceed or retract based on that assessment.[3]

Psychological safety is directly linked to engagement and disengagement, creativity, commitment, and learning behaviors at work. Khan further describes psychological safety as "feeling able to show and employ oneself without fear of negative consequences to self-image, status, or career." Positive work

---

[1] Aranzamendez, Gina, Debbie James, and Robin Toms, (2015). "Finding Antecedents of Psychological Safety: A Step Toward Quality Improvement". *Nursing Forum (Hillsdale), 50*(3) (2015): 171-178.
[2] Edmondson, Amy. "Psychological Safety and Learning Behavior in Work Teams." *Administrative science quarterly* 44, no. 2 (1999): 350-383.
[3] Edmondson, AC. "Learning from failure in health care: frequent opportunities, pervasive barriers" *BMJ Quality & Safety*;13 (2004):ii3-ii9

climates influence the identification and behaviors of all employees, but they hold even greater significance for people of the global majority. Research shows that Black, Indigenous, and people of color (BIPOC) employees seek a work environment that is more affirming of their social identity, making them feel psychologically safe and motivated to meaningfully contribute to the organization. However, the reverse can also be true, further illustrating the importance of psychological safety in such settings.[1]

A lack of psychological safety can look like many things in a fast-paced governmental public health organization. Some may look very similar to experiences in corporate America: ideas presented by Black employees are discarded only to be regaled when brought up by non-Black colleagues; Black employees feel like they always have to "fight" or "struggle" for promotional opportunities that others don't, or they are deathly afraid of the consequences of making a mistake. Others are unique to government: lack of promotional opportunities and resulting disparities in earnings despite supposedly neutral and unbiased hiring and promotional processes; under-resourced programs and initiatives intended for Black communities; and the demonization of Black communities when they reject public health strategies such as vaccination programs. The difference is that in corporate spaces, these instances can decrease productivity and impact the bottom line. In public health, they can delay or altogether disrupt much-needed health care services, negatively impact people's access to health care, increase disease or death (morbidity and mortality in public health speak), and exacerbate long-standing health disparities.

Barbara, a Black Gen X upper manager, talked about how a long-standing lack of resources in her unit (staffed predominantly

[1] SINGH, Barjinder, Doan E WINKEL, and T. T SELVARAJAN. "Managing Diversity at Work: Does Psychological Safety Hold the Key to Racial Differences in Employee Performance?: Getting Diversity at Work to Work." *Journal of occupational and organizational psychology* 86 (2013): 242–263.

with Black workers and located in a predominantly Black community) seriously undermined how work was carried out in her unit. "I once got in trouble with the higher-ups because I missed an important meeting. Thankfully, I was skilled enough to be able to leverage the understaffing of the team to ask for additional positions so that I could be freed to attend high-level meetings. I can't be everywhere at the same time! It took getting in trouble to finally be able to get the staff I needed. Keep in mind that this is a high-need area, so making sure we are appropriately staffed is important to addressing the public health needs of the population."

Janet, an early-career health education professional with a master's degree in public health, shares an experience about a promotion she applied for. "I was first on the hiring list, and I expected to be called for an interview right away. Instead, I started hearing of colleagues who were lower on the list getting called to be interviewed for the position. In a panic, I called my supervisor at the time (a Black woman) to tell her what was happening. She told me to call over there and 'play dumb' by asking if anyone had been hired already because I was first on the list but had not been called for an interview. Soon after, I received an invitation to be interviewed. I was so confused. My name was the first name on the hiring list, and I had the highest score. Why would they overlook me? If I had not advocated for myself, I would not have been considered for the job."

Riley, a millennial health education professional, laments the tone deafness that occurs regarding the health concerns of the Black population in the public health agency where she is employed. "They don't do any substantive engagement in the Black community. No one in the community knows who we are or what we do. Then, when something happens, like a disease outbreak or a pandemic, the expectation is that the community will comply with whatever mandate is handed down. Even worse, they use strategies from an outdated playbook and put the local pastor or community leader in their social media campaigns to encourage people to "fall in line." It never works because it isn't genuine. The only time the Black community hears from the agency is when they want the community to get vaccinated, and then they're confused when the community doesn't comply. There are longstanding trust issues with those sorts of things, and the agency must make a long-term investment to build trust."

What Barbara, Janet, and Riley experienced are the realities of a broken public health system in the United States. Modern American public health is an institution focused on the promotion of health and the prevention of disease in communities. The institution uses data, theory, and other evidence to drive improvements in population health. At its core, public health is a societal effort "to ensure the conditions in which everyone can be healthy.[1] Public health is different from health care in that the focus is on the prevention of disease before treatment is required by the health care system. Additionally, health care is focused on the care of an individual and public health focuses on communities of many types.

Despite its altruistic mission and vision, the development and current practice of the American public health system are rooted in white supremacy culture.[2] Modern public health practice in the United States began in the mid-19th century and was very closely aligned with early urbanization efforts that focused on improving living conditions and housing.[3] There was a tremendous accumulation of knowledge and resources for both healthcare and public health, but disparities in access to both were prevalent. At the time, the primary solutions to health crises that originated from

[1] DeSalvo, Karen B., Y. Claire Wang, Andrea Harris, John Auerbach, Denise Koo, and Patrick O'Carroll. "Public Health 3.0: A Call to Action for Public Health to Meet the Challenges of the 21st Century." *Preventing chronic disease* 14, no. 9 (2017): E78–E78.
[2] Ford, Chandra L., Derek. M. Griffith, Marino A. (Marino Anton) Bruce, and Keon L. Gilbert, eds. *Racism : Science & Tools for the Public Health Professional.* Washington, DC: American Public Health Association, 2019.
[3] Fairchild, Amy L, David Rosner, James Colgrove, Ronald Bayer, and Linda P Fried. "The EXODUS of Public Health What History Can Tell Us About the Future." *American journal of public health (1971)* 100, no. 1 (2010): 54–63.

poor living conditions were to displace and remove Blacks and immigrants.[1]

Despite the growth of public health programs and strategies in the 20th century, Black people's health issues were of no importance to public health. In fact, public health experts of the time believed that the Black community should bear the burden of resolving their issues without any funding or government support.[2] In 1913, only 1 of 9 health departments surveyed in the South reported focusing on Black health issues.

That's why BIPOC public health employees are integral to eliminating health disparities and improving access to care among BIPOC populations.[3] They uphold the entire institution of public health and keep it moving forward. Black public health employees have a significant role in both program development and community engagement with Black populations, who have many of the worst health outcomes in the United States due to systemic oppression and racism.[4] Additionally, the COVID-19 pandemic that disproportionately impacted the Black population and the deaths of Breonna Taylor, Ahmaud Arbery, George Floyd, and others at the hands of law enforcement laid bare the gaps in the provision of services and representation in the public health

[1] Abel, Emily K. "'Only the Best Class of Immigration': Public Health Policy Toward Mexicans and Filipinos in Los Angeles, 1910-1940." *American journal of public health (1971)* 94, no. 6 (2004): 932–939.

[2] LaVeist, Thomas Alexis., and Lydia A. Isaac. *Race, Ethnicity, and Health a Public Health Reader.* 2nd ed. San Francisco: Jossey-Bass, 2012.

[3] Mitchell, Ashley K., Bettye A. Apenteng, and Kwabena G. Boakye. "Examining Factors Associated With Minority Turnover Intention in State and Local Public Health Organizations: The Moderating Role of Race in the Relationship Among Supervisory Support, Job Satisfaction, and Turnover Intention." *Journal of public health management and practice* 28, no. 5 (2022): E768–E777.

[4] Smedley, Brian D, Adrienne Y Stith, and Committee on Understanding and Eliminating Racial and Ethnic Disparities in Health Care. *Unequal Treatment: Confronting Racial and Ethnic Disparities in Health Care. Unequal Treatment: Confronting Racial and Ethnic Disparities in Health Care (with CD).* 1st ed. Washington: National Academies Press, 2002.

workforce.[1] Many of us witnessed, in real time, the manifestation of systemic racism and oppression in how COVID-19 information and resources were shared in our communities. Sadly, I was not surprised at what I witnessed—news only—when low-income stories of vaccine appointments in inner-city neighborhoods being taken by people that live outside of the community and resources provided that were online only, when many living in low-income communities don't have smartphones or Wi-Fi and aren't savvy at navigating the World Wide Web. It was like a page taken out of a centuries-old playbook.

BIPOC employees are needed because we:

- Provide effective health care because we understand what it feels like to be treated poorly in the health care system.
- Improve access to care because we know that access to health care can be the difference between life and death.
- Eliminate health disparities because we know that no one is coming to save us, and we feel a responsibility and obligation to help make a difference in the communities we were born or live in currently.

Despite our potential for impact, it may surprise you to know that public health employees of color leave or wish to leave their jobs at rates higher than their white counterparts. Something happens where their desire to improve the health status of their communities is tamped down and buried under bureaucracy, lack of funding, and halfhearted health programs that do nothing to create lasting change in population health outcomes. Frustration and defeat set in. The irony is that public health is a social justice

---

[1] Travis, Alexis. "Infusing Equity into Organizational Culture at Governmental Public Health Agencies." *Journal of public health management and practice* 29, no. 1 (2023): S12–S13.

institution. One of the foundational premises of public health is that everyone should have access to the resources and opportunities that will afford them a healthy life.

However, the current public health workforce is predominantly white and nearing retirement age. At a critical moment in the history of public health, the institution is struggling with a diversity, equity, and inclusion problem that will render it unable to address the unique needs of a growing and diverse population. At a time when the public craves authenticity and accessibility, Black women in public health are the best equipped to do the work but are becoming disenchanted with the work and choosing other opportunities.

So, what's the solution? It's not entirely feasible to quit a "good government job," especially if you've already spent a significant amount of time there, have family to support, and are looking forward to a pension down the line. In my case, I've passed the 20-year mark in my career and am too close to important milestones to consider leaving now. What I have done is create a space for myself outside of work that allows me to share my public health expertise in meaningful ways *and* could potentially set me up for a career shift after I retire.

**Know what you are getting into, decide in what ways you will make an impact, and decide on an exit strategy if needed.** Governmental public health as an industry operates in the same way as every other system in society. Bias, anti-Blackness, and other forms of oppression are present, despite mission and vision statements that include words like "equity" and phrases like "for all." It is important to understand how these systems and structures work and what part you will play in them. Additionally, you will need to decide what contributions you make are meaningful to you, which might be different from what is considered conventionally successful. For example, the number of people I have helped get into graduate school or find a job are things that I deem successes for me because promotions and pay raises do not often match my work effort. When a staff person tells me I've taught them more in three months about leadership than they've ever learned in their career and that I "saved them," I know that I am successful and am doing the right thing.

**Give yourself credit for the value you create, even when it is not appreciated.** At one point in my career, I was asked to build and implement a large-scale project that created value for not only my place of work but the entire jurisdiction. I managed hundreds of staff, directed the innovation and creation of systems and structures to streamline processes, and responded to urgent directives at a moment's notice. There was an opportunity to be promoted to a managerial role related to this effort, and I was sure I'd get a chance to compete. When that did not happen, I started to question everything about myself. I wondered if the awards and accolades for the project could have been participation trophies. Were they true acknowledgments of the efforts of myself and my team? I doubted my skills, talents, and abilities and wondered if I belonged. Through therapy, self-reflection, and the encouragement of friends and colleagues, I realized that I was not an imposter but had been made to feel that way. I was also able to take stock of the body of work that had been created and the vast impact it had on work operations and the community. The effects of those efforts are still in operation today, a testament to the value I created for my place of work.

**Find or create your support system both at work (where appropriate) and outside of work.** A lot of us aren't interested in having friendships at work, and that's totally understandable. It can be difficult to determine who is safe to confide in with our concerns, fears, and gripes about the job. However, I firmly believe that there is value in carefully and thoughtfully aligning yourself with colleagues who have a shared understanding and experience. One of the reasons to do this is so that you get the mental health boost that comradery provides.

The other benefit is a balance check. Things may be happening to you that have you feeling out of sorts. It is helpful to have colleagues check in on what is happening to be sure what you are experiencing is not an aberration. Over the years, I've called colleagues, and the first words out of my mouth are, "Am I crazy?"

Their response is always "absolutely not; I'm experiencing it too," followed by advice on how to cope. Your "regular" friends are also invaluable. They may not understand your work the way that you do, but they know *you* very well and are often able to offer insight and feedback that is very valuable. In all of this, it is important to remember to make deposits in the friendship bank account, especially when you are making huge withdrawals due to intense work issues. This means, when you are able, checking in on your friends, thanking them for their help, and making plans to celebrate with them. You don't want to wear out your welcome with the people who care about you the most.

**Do things that fill your cup.** One of the ways that I create balance in my life is by practicing self-care (doing my nails is my main self-care activity), contributing to my community by hosting pop-up shops for Black women-owned businesses, serving on boards and commissions, acting as a mentor to students and early career professionals, hosting a weekly video podcast, and generally being a help to anyone that needs it. It's important to build a life beyond your job. As a Gen X'er, I was taught directly and indirectly that one of the ways my worth is determined is my job and that if I work hard and prove myself, I will be rewarded for those efforts. Filling my cup in other ways became very important when things at work didn't happen as anticipated. The other endeavors keep me motivated, inspired, and excited about my life beyond work.

**Consider other ways to share your expertise.** I am starting to see many Black women using their public health expertise to go into business for themselves. Many have acquired many years of experience and have advanced degrees, making consulting a viable career path. Additionally, teaching can be another way to share your expertise and inspire the next generation of public health scholars. I spent almost 15 years teaching public health to undergraduates at private liberal arts colleges, urban universities, and online universities. In each setting, my mission was threefold: to inspire a new generation of public health leaders, teach them the "Black Girl Magic" version of public health that incorporates public health concepts with real-life examples of public health in practice, and leave students with a "social justice lens" through which they see and move through the world.

This is not just a problem for those invested in the institution of public health. We need to be concerned about what is happening because an inadequate and unresponsive public health system impacts us all.

---

**Nicole D. Vick, EdD(c), MPH, CHES**

www.nicoledvick.com

Nicole D. Vick leverages 20+ years as a public health expert, her education, lived experiences, and roles as author, TEDx speaker, trainer, and facilitator to teach, engage, and inspire. She supports small businesses and educates the next generation of public health leaders.

# 10

# EVEN WITH MY MOUTH CLOSED, I STILL SPEAK

## Dr. Natoshia Anderson

I was working on a big project; this was probably mid-career as an engineer. I'm the mechanical engineer of record on this project. We were redesigning a historical building on an army base in Georgia. The design team was meeting the client on the military base to review the project with the commander.

I can tell y'all now, that it was a lot of back and forth just to get on the base, much less who was going to be a part of the project itself. So, the fact that I was a part WAS A BIG DEAL.

That day, the whole engineering design team met with the commander which included me (Black woman) and four white men. The commander, also a white male, comes in late, looks around the room, throws a pen and pad down in front of me, proceeds to his seat and starts the meeting. There is an audible gasp from me and from the other male engineers in the room, yet they don't say anything else. This is the moment. I had a choice, I could let this offense go, pick up the pen and paper and write notes or I could "confront" the commander.

Obviously, I had to do something. The men in the room were all looking at me, and I knew that if I let this slight go, I could expect similar incidents from my team. My grandmother and mother had taught me well when they had told me "You teach people how to treat you."

So, my decision was made. I asked the commander what the pen and pad are for. He said for me to take "notes." Because for him the *only* reason I could be in the room is to take notes. I corrected him, respectfully, by letting him know that I was the mechanical engineer for the project and that if he needed someone to take notes that he would need to have someone from his office come do that for him. He turned all shades of red. He couldn't recover, excused himself and sent his next in line into the meeting to reschedule the meeting.

What does my presence represent when I show up in rooms? It's a power that I've learned to harness and use for good through action, and it's a power that comes with a responsibility to make a difference. This unique form of communication is a result of the rich tapestry of experiences that come with being a Black woman in today's world. It is a reminder that our mere existence challenges norms, stereotypes, and biases.

Growing up, I often heard the phrase, "Actions speak louder than words." Little did I know how profoundly this idea would resonate with me as I navigated through a world that often underestimated, marginalized, and silenced people who looked like me. But I was determined to let my actions be a testament to my strength, my resilience, and my unwavering commitment to change.

My earliest memories of this power come from my childhood, where I observed how my mother carried herself. She was a woman of few words, but her actions spoke volumes. She worked tirelessly to provide for our family, never complaining about the challenges she faced. She taught me that perseverance and hard work could transcend any obstacle. Her silent strength became a source of inspiration for me, a template for the kind of woman I wanted to become.

As I entered spaces beyond my home, I realized that my mere presence disrupted preconceived notions and stereotypes.

My brown skin, my natural hair, and my proud identity as a Black woman challenged the status quo, and it didn't require me to utter a word. In a world where systemic racism persisted, it became clear that my existence alone was a form of resistance.

I realized that I carried a responsibility to not only represent myself but also my community. This responsibility, however, was not a burden but an opportunity. I had the power to challenge biases and promote understanding, even in spaces that were initially hostile or ignorant. My actions were my weapon against injustice.

I learned this at a pretty young age as I navigated integrating a school in the early 1970's with my siblings and two other brave Black boys and girls. We learned that "we were all we had" in school. I learned this in the neighborhood where we were the only people of color. It mattered that we were people of integrity. People of principles. We are good people. It mattered. We didn't have to say anything at all. We just lived our lives and stayed to ourselves. We knew that people were watching us; in fact, they placed signs and threw bricks through the windows of our house to let us know that they were indeed watching us.

Even though it was a scary time, we understood that we couldn't show fear. I learned then that my parents and my siblings were revolutionary.

One of the most profound lessons I learned was the power of solidarity. When Black women come together, our collective actions can create waves of change. The sisterhood and support within our community are unparalleled. Together, we amplify each other's voices and take collective action to address issues ranging from racial inequality to gender discrimination.

Through education and self-awareness, I discovered the importance of allyship and advocacy. I began to engage in conversations that mattered, even when they were uncomfortable. I joined organizations dedicated to fighting for social justice, and I used my skills and talents to contribute to the causes I believed in. I realized that my actions had the potential to inspire others to join the fight for a more equitable world.

But it wasn't just about advocating for change externally. I also had to unpack my own biases and prejudices. I learned that personal growth and self-reflection were integral parts of using my power for good. It was not enough to be silent in the face of injustice; I had to actively work to unlearn harmful beliefs and actively promote inclusivity.

Throughout my journey, I've encountered countless challenges and setbacks. There have been moments when I've felt weary, when it seemed like the world would never change. But I've also witnessed progress, moments of unity, and glimpses of a better future. I've seen how even the smallest actions can create a ripple effect, eventually leading to significant change.

As a Black woman, my power to speak through my actions has become a source of strength, resilience, and hope. I've learned that I don't need to raise my voice to make an impact, but when I do choose to speak, my words carry the weight of lived experiences and a vision for a more just world. I've learned that even with my mouth closed, I still speak. Loudly and proudly. I'm committed to using that power to create a better tomorrow for all.

## THE POWER OF PRESENCE

In a world that often tries to silence or marginalize Black voices, the power of our presence is undeniable. It's a power rooted in history, in the strength and resilience of generations who came before us, who fought against the chains of oppression and worked tirelessly to carve out a place for us in society.

Even when I enter a space with my mouth closed, my presence tells a story. It tells a story of a Black woman who has overcome obstacles, who has achieved against the odds, and who refuses to be invisible. It's a story of pride, of identity, and of the knowledge that my existence alone is a form of resistance.

During my early years as an engineer, I made a conscious effort to prioritize learning and observation in the various professional spaces and meetings I attended. People often questioned why I didn't actively participate by asking questions or speaking up, especially in contrast to my white colleagues who were quite vocal. However, I chose a different path for a couple of specific reasons. First, I didn't have a clear sense of whom I could trust in those settings. Second, I struggled to decipher the unspoken dynamics and rules governing those spaces, so I adopted a watchful approach to see how everything unfolded.

Additionally, my introverted nature played a role, as I didn't initially possess the skills to effectively network and navigate large gatherings. I did my best with the resources and abilities I had at the time. Unfortunately, this led to a misunderstanding that I was antisocial during that period, which ultimately had a negative impact on my career progression within that company.

Over time, higher-ups concluded that I lacked ambition because my supervisors conveyed the false message that I hadn't made any effort to connect with my colleagues or engage with peers. This characterization, though untrue, became a stigma that I couldn't shake off. My silence in meetings and the absence of a robust social network were interpreted as shortcomings, overshadowing the quality of my work. Essentially, they judged me as a person without truly knowing me. I cannot tell you how many times this same thing played itself out over the course of the first five years of my engineering career.

Then I made the career transition from engineering to higher education. I jumped into the world of higher education with both feet. I served on committees, soaked up information, talked with my colleagues both in and out of my department, made some friends and some enemies along the way. I was one of two women in my whole department, and I was the ONLY woman of color faculty member in the department. All the other faculty of color were in the Arts and Sciences and Business divisions.

This was so like my experiences when I was a practicing engineer. I had to make my own way there too. It seemed that there were some, even in my department, that were a bit threatened by me. I was later told that I had too much confidence. Let that sink in for a bit. I had TOO MUCH confidence.

And when those that were already threatened by me found out that I was in the process of obtaining my doctorate, all HELL broke loose. One of the people that was most threatened by me turned out to be my Department Chair. She had a STEM background as well and had been a Dept. Chair for six years when I showed up. She was well established at the college.

One would think that we would've been close. What I didn't know was that she didn't like to be outshone. She didn't like that I was smart and could and did stand up to her when she was wrong. She didn't like that I was doing things in my department that allowed us to be noticed. She didn't like that my colleagues liked me and wanted to collaborate with me.

These were all things that hadn't happened before in the department. Before my arrival, the department, and especially, my program had a high turnover rate. But here I was...sticking like glue and getting noticed by the upper administration. She'd whisper things to me about upper administration, thinking that I'd take her word for who they were. I couldn't form my own opinions.

When I'd started getting noticed from upper administration, my evaluations, which had all been excellent in the years before, came to need improvement. Yet, I'd done nothing different from the year before. She blatantly told me once that I was "getting too big," for the department. I either had to be a team member or find a new team. My time off requests went ignored, "got lost," or were denied. My requests for equipment or software upgrades were denied. Conferences were denied. Any type of professional development opportunities was being turned down. She even told me that I couldn't go talk to students at our local high school as that would have me leaving the campus.

She got irate at me once, when a conference proposal that I and another colleague put in was accepted to a national conference. I asked our grants office to find money for me to attend. They did. She made every attempt to stop my colleague and me from going. She went to the dean and VP about this issue and told them that I went behind her back to put in the proposal, therefore I shouldn't be allowed to attend. I went to that conference and delivered that presentation and the college received national attention.

## THE WEIGHT OF STEREOTYPES

I am acutely aware of the stereotypes and biases that society attaches to people who look like me. These stereotypes can be suffocating, limiting, and deeply hurtful. But I've come to realize that even when I don't say a word, I have the power to challenge and shatter these stereotypes. Walking into a STEM classroom or laboratory, I have often been greeted with curious glances and raised eyebrows. The hallowed halls of science and technology, while seemingly impartial, are not immune to the biases that permeate society. Being one of the few Black women in the room, my mere presence often defies stereotypes and challenges preconceived notions about who belongs in STEM. My existence became a testament to breaking barriers, a living embodiment of resilience.

In a room full of thermodynamic equations and mechanical diagrams, my silent presence became a statement—a counter-narrative to the stereotypes that sought to confine me. Every step I took was a resonance of determination, a reminder that excellence knows no boundaries. The quiet power of a Black woman in STEM lies in the unspoken promise of possibility. My mere existence becomes a statement—a declaration that I refuse to be silenced by prejudice and discrimination. Every class success was a testament to my willpower to make it to the next.

Being a Black woman engineer hasn't been easy. I wouldn't change the choice I made even though it has brought many challenges. There is this belief that we only got here through affirmative action, or that we lack the competence or capability to be in STEM. That as Black women, we didn't earn our degrees. Well, I am here to tell you that I didn't spend five and a half years at Georgia's Southern Polytech State University (now known as Kennesaw State University) being the only woman and often only minority in my classes, being ostracized and picked lasted, being left out of group chats and meetings, and having to be my own advisor when the advisor assigned to me refused to see me. I earned my degree. I barely got out, but I did, indeed, get out. You know what they call a person with a 2.2 GPA and a degree in mechanical engineering? A Mechanical Engineer. Yep, they do! These stereotypes are harmful and have led to the underrepresentation of Black women in STEM.

- According to the National Science Foundation (NSF), Black women remain underrepresented in STEM fields. In 2019, they represented only 2.9% of the employed workforce in computer and mathematical sciences and 3.6% in engineering.[1]

- A study published in the Journal *Sex Roles* found that Black women in STEM often face double stereotypes based on both their gender and race, which can impact their career advancement and opportunities.[2]

- Research has shown that implicit bias can affect hiring decisions. A study by the National Academy of Sciences found that science faculty rated the same application materials more positively when they were attributed to a male candidate compared to a female one, regardless of the applicant's actual gender. Science faculty's subtle gentle biases favor male students.[3]

- In STEM fields, there is a gender pay gap, and this disparity is even more significant for Black women. Data from the American Association of University

[1] Deitz, Elizabeth Grieco and Steven. n.d. "Diversity and STEM: Women, Minorities, and Persons With Disabilities 2023 | NSF - National Science Foundation." https://ncses.nsf.gov/pubs/nsf23315/report/the-stem-workforce.

[2] Sendze, Margery S. 2022. "I Can't Quit: Experiences of Black Women in STEM Professions." Journal of Career Assessment 31 (2): 377–96. https://doi.org/10.1177/10690727221118696.

[3] Moss-Racusin, Corinne A., John F. Dovidio, Victoria L. Brescoll, Mark Graham, and Jo Handelsman. 2012. "Science Faculty's Subtle Gender Biases Favor Male Students." Proceedings of the National Academy of Sciences of the United States of America 109 (41): 16474–79. https://doi.org/10.1073/pnas.1211286109.

Women (AAUW) indicates that Black women in STEM earn, on average, 66 cents for every dollar earned by White men.[1]

It's important to recognize that while there are challenges and stereotypes, Black women in STEM continue to make significant contributions to their fields and inspire future generations. Efforts to break down barriers, increase representation, and combat stereotypes are essential to create more inclusive STEM environments.

Stereotypes are not based on fact, and if you rely on them, they can and often do lead to all sorts of misunderstandings and biases in the workplace. For years, I grappled with how to address these stereotypes effectively and not become them. I realized that words alone would not do the trick; some sort of action needs to be taken.

I started by first excelling in my studies. For me, leaving no room for doubt about my competency. I sought out mentors and allies who spoke to my abilities and amplified my voice when necessary. I also took time to work through the trauma experienced at college and the workplace to get really clear on who I am and who I am not. I can challenge them by being unapologetically myself, by refusing to conform to someone else's idea of who I should be. I can challenge them by excelling in my chosen field, by being a leader, and by showing the world that Black women are not defined by the narrow boxes that society tries to put us in.

## Using My Powers for Good

As I've gotten older, I've come to realize what my power truly is. It's a power that calls for action, for advocacy, and for change. I've learned to use my influence to lift those who are still struggling, to advocate for policies that address racial and gender

---

[1] "The Simple Truth About the Pay Gap." 2023. AAUW : Empowering Women Since 1881. October 16, 2023.
https://www.aauw.org/resources/research/simple-truth/.

disparities, and to challenge systems of oppression wherever I encounter them. As I honed my skills and navigated the intricate web of STEM dynamics, I realized that my silent power was a force to be reckoned with. It wasn't about fitting into predefined molds; it was about reshaping the narrative. I discovered the strength in mentorship, community building, and uplifting others along the journey.

As I progressed in my STEM journey, I realized that my visibility was a powerful tool also. It wasn't just about occupying physical space in STEM but also about the impact my presence could have on others. Representation matters, and by being visible in STEM, I was inadvertently becoming a source of inspiration for those who felt marginalized or doubted their place in this field.

I've joined movements, spoken at rallies, and used my platform to bring attention to the issues that matter most to me and my community. I've mentored young Black women, helping them to recognize their own power and potential. I've used my power to effect change in the workplace, pushing for diversity and inclusion initiatives that benefit everyone.

It's why I started my entrepreneurial efforts. It's my goal to help young Black women in STEM who have encountered detrimental DEI issues and want to know how to handle them. It's why I host the podcast STEMming in Stilettos, so young women can hear and learn from the stories of other minority women in STEM. We are in this together and we can learn from each other. Here is the thing; We can't keep our stories hidden and hope that everything will get better.

From the moment we step into a room, we carry with us the weight of history, the legacies of those who came before us. Our mere presence challenges the status quo, disrupts norms, and demands acknowledgment. We are living, breathing embodiments of our ancestors' dreams and aspirations. Our silence is an assertion of our existence, a proclamation of our worthiness, and a reminder of our humanity. Because even with my mouth closed, I still speak.

But silence is not enough; it must be accompanied by action. We must harness the power of our presence to effect change, to dismantle systems of oppression, and to uplift our communities. It is in our actions that we truly amplify our voices, making them impossible to ignore.

- **Educating Ourselves:** Knowledge is a potent weapon, and we must arm ourselves with it. We must educate ourselves about our history, our culture, and the struggles that have brought us to this point. Understanding the roots of oppression empowers us to challenge and dismantle it. I do this by reading books. Here are three of my favorites:
    i. Black, Brown, Bruised: How Racialized STEM Education Stifles Innovation by Ebony Omotola McGee
    ii. You're More Than a Diversity Hire: Women in STEM by Angelique Adams, PhD.
    iii. Letters To My Sisters in Engineering by Brittany Wilkins
- **Building Bridges:** Silence can be isolating but we are never truly alone. We must actively seek out allies and build bridges with those who share our commitment to justice and equality. Together, we can amplify our voices and create lasting change.
- **Leading by Example:** Our actions can inspire others to join the fight for justice. By taking the lead in our communities, workplaces, and homes, we demonstrate the power of resilience and determination. We become beacons of hope for future generations.
- **Advocating for Change:** Let our actions shout for justice. We must engage in advocacy, whether through grassroots organizing, policy reform, or community outreach. Our actions can influence laws, policies, and societal norms.

- **Mentoring and Empowering:** As Black women, we must uplift and mentor younger generations, nurturing their potential to become powerful agents of change. By sharing our wisdom and experiences, we ensure a legacy of strength and resilience.
  - iv. P.O.L.I.S.H. Mentoring with James Bumpas
  - v. Society of Black Scientists and Engineers
  - vi. National Society of Black Engineers
  - vii. Minority Women in Science
  - viii. Black Girls Code
- **Caring for Ourselves:** Our journey is long and challenging, and self-care is essential. By prioritizing our physical and emotional well-being, we strengthen our ability to effect change. Self-care is not a sign of weakness but a manifestation of our commitment to the cause.
- **Creating Spaces for Our Voices:** Sometimes, we must create our own spaces where our voices can be heard. Whether through art, literature, or grassroots initiatives, we have the power to shape narratives and challenge stereotypes.
  - ix. Write your own blog.
  - x. Start your own podcast.
  - xi. Publish a LinkedIn newsletter.

## CONCLUSION

My experiences have given me the wisdom to know that my silence is my superpower. And in my silence, my presence is also a power that I can use for the good of my people. My presence, my actions, and my advocacy all send a powerful message to the world. By actively engaging with my community and working toward a positive change, I am making a lasting impact. I am a force to be reckoned with, and I will not be silenced. My journey to learn to use my powers for good through action has been a lifelong one, and it continues every day.

I am determined to change the narrative. We will not be silent or be silenced. Our stories must be told. I'll keep telling them. Our journey is one of resilience, strength, and unwavering determination. Even with our mouths closed, we continue to speak volumes, inspiring others to join us in the pursuit of a more equitable world.

**Natoshia Anderson, Ed. D.**
www.drtoshia.co
Dr. Natoshia Anderson dedicates her work to creating equal STEM opportunities, empowering, and advocating for women of color to find their voice and stand out. An engineer, educator, career consultant, speaker, and author, she partners with individuals and orgs to enact change at all levels — from increasing youth awareness to sparking conversations on confidence, leadership, and advocacy.

# 11

## ESCALATOR BLUES
### An Emotional Trauma Unpacked

SHAREDA M. ROLLINS

I'm sure you've heard others express the sentiment, *'I'm used to being the only one or one of a few."* Let me assure you that it never gets easier, no matter how frequently you experience it. Whether it's in college, during an internship, grad school, or navigating the corporate landscape, the overwhelming sense of solitude, isolation, and the persistent feeling of an 'us and them' dynamic can be suffocating and deeply triggering. It leaves behind a lingering pain that ebbs and flows, resurfacing with different situations that evoke memories and emotions from not-too distant past experiences.

Being a Black woman navigating work and relationships in a predominantly white space is subject to trauma all its own. Her words are often unspoken or silenced, yet today she is emerging louder, more passionate and with more emotionally intelligent thinking and decision-making ability than ever before. Read her stories of tragedy and triumph. See her. See yourself. Empower her. Empower yourself. All through her stories.

## WHAT HAPPENED TO YOU?

During my graduate school years, it was particularly disheartening when projects were complete and grades were calculated, and I found myself defending my good grades outside one of our classrooms at the school of education. As my classmates, primarily white women, shared results, laughter, and dismissive comments came hurling my way: 'You got good grades because the teacher liked you' or 'you were the teacher's pet for sure. ' Like arrows, the words pierced through me. It was an assault of a different kind. One that I had not experienced before. These were mature adults with jobs, careers, and even responsibility for protecting our children's social and emotional well-being in the classroom; yet, here in this moment, they take no account for my or their words. I stood caught between defense and perplexity, forever traumatized by the moment.

"No, ma'am", I thought as I began to express the sentiment of my heart, which was that I had worked hard, burning the midnight oil, juggling teaching, grading, and volunteering, all while enduring evenings away from my children as I studied in coffee shops, hotel lobbies, and restaurants after an exhausting day's work. My entire family made a sacrifice to support my pursuit of a master's degree. To reduce my accomplishment solely to the favoritism of my white teacher was more than an insult. I often think of this moment and wish I had been louder and more pronounced in my conviction. I said my peace but was it heard? I am not sure. Did it evoke change? I am not sure. Reliving these memories brings forth anger and disappointment in people. The memory is just one of many examples of how Black women must defend themselves from micro-aggressive behaviors and bullying tactics. What would have been better is if one of the people in that group had had enough guts to stand up for me. However, I have learned through my study that white women, who are also marginalized in workspaces, can unfortunately end up being the ones who are marginalizing others.[1]

As a Black woman, why should I have to defend my successes? When do we get the chance to simply revel in our achievements without having to be on the defensive? I yearn to lower my guard and ease the tension in my shoulders. It takes a lot of emotional fortitude to navigate environments where white people predominate. My classmates were casting a light that shines on their privilege. The men were not challenged for getting good grades; they did not challenge each other for one having a higher grade than the other. So, why was I the subject of this blatant attempt to diminish my success? I may never know.

"Microaggressions may seem insignificant when viewed as isolated incidents. But when they occur day after day—as they often do—their impact builds up and takes a toll. Whether intentional or unintentional, these insults and invalidations signal disrespect. It's hard for any employee to bring out their best self when they're often underestimated and slighted. Women who experience microaggressions are three times more likely to regularly think about leaving their job than those who don't." [2]

Monnica Williams, PhD board-certified licensed clinical psychologist and professor, shared in a recorded speech for the University of Toronto entitled *"Racial Trauma: How Racism can cause PTSD"* a list of multiple forms of racism, such as aversive racism, when people support racial equality outwardly but internally have conflicting negative feelings about people of color and who act just like other racists when others are not looking.[3]

In my case, her explanation led me to the definition of covert racism, which was more directly connected to my scenario and defined it as patronizing statements and backhanded

[1] Barratt, Bianca. 2020. "The Microaggressions towards Black Women You Might Be Complicit in at Work." *Forbes*, June 19, 2020.
[2] "The State of Black Women in Corporate America." n.d. Lean In. https://leanin.org/research/state-of-black-women-in-corporate-america.
[3] Factor-Inwentash Faculty of Social Work. 2022. "Racial Trauma: How Racism Can Cause PTSD, with Monnica Williams

comments known more commonly as microaggressions. [1] This covert form of racism, which would likely be denied if I had challenged my peers since, according to Williams, is a common practice by whites to limit their definition of racism to blatant acts. My peers could no longer hold in their ideology that I did not deserve to be an A student and once a single person spoke out, the others felt empowered to form agreement. This was not "old-fashioned" racist behavior. It was hidden under laughter and wrapped in weeks of friendly teamwork and collaboration that gave them access to me as an individual. The experience was deeply personal and left me with a feeling of betrayal.

It is likely that if I had stayed in education long enough, one or more of my peers would have become a colleague or leader above or alongside me at an educational institution in my city. Their actions showed that they were ok with me being in class, supporting their ideas and making suggestions on work products, but the line was drawn when my success surpassed theirs in class outcomes. When the prejudiced actions of leaders within organizations have a substantial and detrimental effect on the professional advancement of Black women who have shown consistent commitment, ethical work and other quality workplace characteristics, it is referred to by Dr. Kecia M. Thomas, a distinguished professor at the University of Georgia, as "Pet to Threat." This term resonated with me and grieved me, as I know that ultimately what my classroom peers exhibited could become the training ground for their future pet-to-threat behavior. It's like love bombing for the workplace.

Employers must make equity, racial healing, and emotional intelligence front runners in corporate culture. No, my experience above was not with leaders who had input on my career, but peers can become someone's boss and certainly play a critical role in how men and women of color are perceived and promoted. The

---

[1] Factor-Inwentash Faculty of Social Work. 2022. "Racial Trauma: How Racism Can Cause PTSD, with Monnica Williams

unfortunate truth is that we often need the allyship of our counterparts to advance in roles and pay. We all have had friends who have spent years working for a company to be turned down multiple times for jobs that secure the bag and even be required to train the person who takes on the role. Statistics show we are better suited with allies, but how do companies insure allyship with the attack on diversity, equity and inclusion efforts (DEI)? A 2017 Harvard Business Review (HBR) study shared that black employees hired through a referral process saw an increased number of promotions compared to black employees without a referral. Confirmation that yes, allyship is needed to thwart the larger systemic issues at play.[1]

## HOW DID THIS EXPERIENCE IMPACT YOU IN CORPORATE AMERICA?

It was the first day of work. I had quit my job as a teacher to pursue work in corporate America. Schoolgirl excitement ran through my body as I arrived early to my work site. I found a place to sit nestled at the bottom of a set of escalator stairs. In this space, I could see people coming and going. Since I was a child, I have found great enjoyment in people watching. There are profound lessons to be learned when you observe people. It is perhaps this affinity that has led me to work in people-centric professions like training and championing emotional intelligence.

As I sat, a few other early birds straddled in for new hire orientation. Then a few more and a few more. The visual was art in motion, like a time lapse as the trickle moved from a few people to what felt like droves of people. Then it happened, just before 8 a.m. I peered up to watch two rows of escalators flow toward me, delivering people to me at eye level one after the other. What started out as a gentle smile with eager anticipation shifted. I

---

[1] Merluzzi, Jennifer. 2017. "Research: Black Employees Are More Likely to Be Promoted When They Were Referred by Another Employee." Harvard Business Review. April 11, 2017.

nodded good morning to those who made eye contact as a show of acknowledgement but suddenly my smile faded, my heart rate began to rise, and my eyes got bigger. In reflection, now I know that I was in a full-on panic attack for the first time in my life. The whiteness had engulfed me, and it was an event that I would describe as drowning in the moment. I had to talk myself down. "Relax, Shareda, take a few deep breaths, and breathe, girl, breathe," would be stated softly under my breath as I affirmed myself with self-talk that all would be well. My world was shaking on a day that I had been praying for. "You have got to maintain your composure; you can do this!"

I have always been the only one among the few and that is not new, as I stated earlier. McKinsey and workforce.[1] Realities like this are emotionally draining. Such a small company reports in a 2021 study that African Americans (and Asians) make up only 14% of the population and must always prove themselves and their value. This day at the escalator, it was nearly more than I could handle. In hopes of self-regulating, I checked in with myself, asking directly, "What is wrong?" My heart responded, "I do not see myself." I was not there—a middle-aged, married, Black woman who had birthed three kids. The woman who was looking for her next career moves to show up bold, creative, and with years of wisdom. The team player who wanted to collaborate and expand her work territory by using her degrees, experiences, pain, and all that she was and wanted to be. You know, show up authentically me. I did not see her. Where was she? She was the one who longed to change her life. She was the one who believed in God for a supernatural shift for her family. I sat and watched as if in a trance. She did not come down those stairs. Nor did I lock eyes with her Latina, African, or Island sister, young or old. This moment left a profound imprint on my psyche, and it weighed on my shoulders for years to come.

The escalator blues are not just my experience. In years of

---

[1] "Race in the Workplace: The Black Experience in the US Private Sector." 2021. *McKinsey & Company*.

conversations with colleagues and friends, I have come to know that they have faced ongoing psychological experiences looking for themselves and/or defending themselves in spaces occupied by the historic majority. Peruse LinkedIn on any given day, and there is a story of grief, resilience, or escape. I learned a great emotional lesson from my escalator moment, and it was that I had not outlived, outworked, out educated, or outgrown the psychological response of being 'the only or the few'. My new degree and new career did not prepare, protect, or absolve me from being a Black woman working in a place where I am the minority. In that instant, I was taken right back to the school of education, and I saw myself in a space where I would have to defend myself all over again.

This reality became even more starkly evident in the wake of the George Floyd incident in our country. It underscored that the struggles and challenges faced in those moments on the escalator or those on the college campus are not isolated incidents but part of a broader systemic issue. While George Floyd's tragedy was a glaring manifestation, it merely echoed the persistent struggles many individuals of color face daily in environments. It reminded me that our battles for recognition and fair treatment continue but are impacting our lives now in a way that we can give words through self-awareness and self-reflective tools that position us to give voice. I did not have the words before. I did not have the voice before.

I seized an opportunity to engage in a pivotal conversation within my company, specifically addressing hundreds of my white colleagues in the aftermath of the George Floyd incident in our nation. I candidly expressed my emotions—feelings of distress and confusion at the escalators on my first day of work for a company with thousands of employees and only a fraction that looked like me—and issued a challenge to my coworkers: to stand as allies and advocates in spaces where the voices of Black and brown individuals might be sidelined, downplayed, or silenced. The dialogue was empowering for me, recognizing that my voice and leadership possessed the potential to spark transformative impact.

This moment of sharing resembled a brief respite for my weary black spirit. I needed that rest. We all need rest.

Numerous companies had begun opening doors to transparent conversations on race and trauma. However, it is imperative that these instances do not merely serve as hollow gestures or marketing ploys toward a superficial sense of change. Companies must develop concrete plans for systemic transformation, ensuring that their black employees are not subjected to the psychological anguish that can perpetuate in the workplace. The Washington Post reported that 1.4 million Black Americans reported higher numbers of depression and anxiety a week after his death, using the George Floyd incident as a barometer for minority health.[1]

This represents reported cases; what about the cases that do not get reported and are buried under the deceiving label of "resilience"? Without structural changes, opportunities for dialogue remain steppingstones in healing journeys but fall short of generating the impactful transformation required at the necessary pace. Furthermore, one must acknowledge the negative racist experiences of Black men and women as actual psychological trauma for it to not be dismissed as our issue alone.

Trauma is defined by the Oxford Dictionary as an experience that is deeply distressing or disturbing to a person.[2] I'm not a therapist or trained in a clinical area that qualifies me to diagnose myself or others, but I know without a shadow of a doubt that my experiences in college, graduate school, and working on all white teams are real and every incident changes you. They can be heavy, hard to identify and explain, and magnified when you enter positions of perceived or actual power. At first glance, you and I could fit quite a few things into this condensed definition of trauma, but the impact of racism and racist behaviors needs to find a place for assessment in the mental health field. While this task is

---

[1] Fowers, Alyssa, and William Wan. 2020. "Depression and Anxiety Spiked among Black Americans after George Floyd's Death." *Washington Post*, June 12, 2020.
[2] "Trauma." n.d. Https://Www.Apa.Org.

still difficult to construct today, Monnica Williams' work is championing it by developing an interview tool for mental health practitioners to validate the racialized experiences of people of color.[1]

## HOW DID YOU NAVIGATE?

Emotional intelligence plays a crucial role in navigating our majority-led communities and workplaces. It involves understanding and managing our emotions effectively, recognizing others' perspectives, and harnessing these insights to build meaningful connections. My experiences with people in the corporate landscape and my innate love of observing the human dynamic led me to practice implementing the pillars of emotional intelligence. I yearned to better understand the teams of people I worked alongside and how I interacted with them based on who they presented themselves to be. This process has given me and my teams a voice to share and understand each other in ways that foster peace and joy—foundations for larger conversations and gateways to change. My colleagues in this anthology will write very deep and heartbreaking accounts of trauma in the workplace, and as readers, you may find yourself resonating from the place of the abused or the abuser. Either way, we all need a plan to survive and cope while we work toward a transformational systemic shift in the corporate landscape.

If you are by chance a member of the current majority, I challenge you to take every story in this anthology to heart as you find your path to support and allyship. Investigate how racially charged workplace behaviors can lead to panic attacks, anxiety, and distress in your Black and brown peers.

My brothers and sisters, for you, I share the following methods I use to navigate the corporate landscape despite the weight of traumatic experiences. These are not individualized

---

[1] "Racial Trauma Research." n.d. Monnica Williams. Accessed February 2, 2024. https://www.monnicawilliams.com/racial-trauma-readings.php.

resolutions but tips to apply broadly, often require pairing with other strategies to be effective and are undoubtedly not a substitute for medical attention to manage your mental health. Transparently, I have paired these with therapy, a newfound love for mental rest, and a bold courage not to be silent. Developing a heightened level of emotional intelligence is necessary and should be regarded as the best life practice.

### NAVIGATING SUCCESS THROUGH EMOTIONAL INTELLIGENCE

**Self-Awareness:** On that life-changing first day at work, sitting by the escalator, I felt a rush of emotions I couldn't ignore. My heart raced, and panic threatened to overwhelm me. However, I recognized the signs of distress. I took a moment to talk myself down, reminding myself to breathe and maintain composure despite the internal chaos. This awareness of my emotions allowed me to navigate the situation more calmly. Understand your emotions, strengths, and limitations. Acknowledge how situations affect you and be mindful of your responses.

**Empathy:** I am familiar with feeling unseen and invisible—I understand what it's like not to see yourself reflected in a space. That realization sparked a deeper sense of empathy within me. I began recognizing and understanding the experiences of others who might feel similarly marginalized, fostering connections based on shared feelings of exclusion. I no longer sit back and say nothing, but I raise questions and draw attention to situations that could be overlooked. I have purposely developed relationships with my white and diverse colleagues to build allies and give them a path to understanding and discussing complex safety issues. Develop the ability to understand and share the feelings of others. This can foster more meaningful connections and a deeper understanding of diverse perspectives.

**Resilience:** The weight of that grad school moment compounded other incidents where I had been demoralized, lied on and gaslit in the workplace. The escalator meltdown showed me that I had not personally acknowledged and reflected on how

I needed to protect my mind from these workplace experiences. Resilience is not about withstanding, as the definition could imply, but about recovery. After the tears and wise counsel (therapy), I embrace each situation as a lesson, not just a lesson for me. It made me stronger and more determined than before to exercise a bigger voice in the workplace so my colleagues could understand my lens and experiences. Cultivate resilience to bounce back from circumstances as learning experiences and use them to grow stronger and teach others.

**Adaptability:** Adaptability has been a guiding trait in my approach. Growing up, I internalized the saying, "When a person shows you who they are, believe it." With time, I evolved it into a personal philosophy: "When people show you who they are, believe it and act accordingly." Understanding the thought process of those I collaborate with is crucial. Over the course of working closely with individuals, their true colors emerge—their strengths, weaknesses, and work ethics.

My adaptability hinges on reacting solely to observable actions or words. I refrain from making assumptions or speculations, recognizing that actions carry more weight than words. It's about discerning the evidence in every situation. This philosophy aligns with the essence of being open to change, embracing diverse perspectives, and tailoring my approach to engage effectively with different personalities. Be flexible and open to change. Embrace different perspectives and adapt your approach to connect with diverse individuals.

**Effective Communication:** The students in my class in graduate school could have gotten a good slurry of choice words from me but instead, I stood on business, as the culture declares. I confirmed very proudly that I earned my grades and that they had no right to think otherwise. I gave voice right in the moment, not as an afterthought and maintained my credibility and decorum in the process. I lost nothing in telling them my position but gained everything as I filled my personal power bucket. Hone your communication skills to express yourself clearly and empathetically. Listen actively and foster an environment conducive to open dialogue.

**Relationship Management:** Navigating conflicts and challenges demanded an understanding of emotions, both mine and those of my colleagues. By acknowledging these emotions and managing them constructively, I endeavored to build positive connections despite differing viewpoints. The training "Crucial Conversations" was an explosive idea for how to change my perspective and corresponding response to conflict. Sometimes anger and outrage are what the doctor ordered but as a matter of practice, I start with civility. Build and maintain positive relationships by understanding others' emotions and navigating conflicts constructively.

Emotional intelligence isn't just a personal trait; it's a skill set that can be developed and honed over time. The above emotional intelligence tips have been pivotal in my journey, not just as principles to follow but as guiding lights through the complexities of community, home, and work. They've helped me not only navigate challenges but also work towards creating a more inclusive and supportive environment for myself and those around me.

In short, there must be a collective effort to create environments where all individuals, regardless of race, can thrive authentically. So, let's be clear: merely "surviving" in the workplace should never be the goal. Each of us needs a healthy dose of emotional vitality. It's the cure to the Elevator Blues.

**Shareda Rollins, M.Ed**

Shareda Rollins, M.Ed. is a dynamic speaker, trainer, and people development leader who inspires others to grow through self-awareness and emotional wellness. As a leader with Oracle Health at the time of print and founder of Rollins Consulting Services, she empowers teams to strengthen connection, communication, and purpose. Her work reflects a guiding belief that emotionally healthy people build stronger teams and stronger communities.

This chapter is adapted from the book entitled, *God & A Plan.*

# 12

## INTENT VS. IMPACT
### Unmasking Microaggressions

WENDY T. TALLEY

Don't let "white folks" see you as some ignorant Black girl.

"Make sure you put on your white girl voice because you don't want them to know you are all Black."

"Let me put this wig on so these folks can stop asking about my braids and how long it took to do it."

I am so f\*\*king tired of waking up and having to figure out how to stop my white co-workers from asking me questions about the Black race. I am not the spokesperson for 7.8 billion Black people in the world.

"I am sorry; that was not my intent; I was merely asking for your opinion."

INTENT VS. IMPACT

Racial microaggressions are brief and commonplace daily verbal, behavioral, or environmental indignities, whether intentional or unintentional, that communicate hostile, derogatory, or harmful racial slights and insults toward people of color.[1] A widespread undercurrent of microaggressions resonates through the experiences of professionals of color. The phrase "that was not my intent" has regrettably been transformed into a shield, a linguistic barricade wielded to deflect accountability for actions that secretly spread racism within the workplace.

This chapter embarks on a deeply emotional exploration, diving further into the elaborate layers of common racial microaggressions that black professionals routinely encounter. In doing so, it aims to illuminate the subtle, yet profoundly impactful ways racism persists within the corporate realm. As we navigate the elaborate web of corporate culture, it becomes evident that the landscape is far from neutral. The echoes of microaggressions — those subtle verbal and non-verbal slights that sideline and belittle — create a difference that reverberates through the daily experiences of professionals of color.

I know those reading this chapter have heard these statements: "No, where are you really from?" "Are all Black women shaped like that?" "You're so articulate for someone from your background." "You're the diversity hire, right?" These microaggressions, often dismissed as unintentional, serve as subtle agents that perpetuate an environment where racism can take root and thrive. I aim to unravel these elaborate threads, exposing the covert nature of microaggressions and their growing impact on the professional lives of Black employees and leaders.

*** 

I landed a job with a company established by a big-shot celebrity right out of undergraduate school. I was nervous and scared. It was my first "real adult" job right out of college. I knew I was ready, and all that hard work would pay off. All I could think about was saving money to get my place and moving out of my

---

[1] McCallaghan, Sean. "Work-place diversity climate: Its association with racial microaggressions and employee work-place well-being." Journal of Psychology in Africa 32, no. 6 (2022): 560-568.

parent's home. I also like partying with my girls without worrying about the bill. BIG GIRL STUFF!

Here is the catch: I knew I had to work twice as hard as my Caucasian counterparts to prove I belonged. The office vibe was a mix of white supervisors and a Latina co-worker, and I quickly learned the unwritten rules of survival around "those white folks," as my mom would say.

Sitting here with my eyes closed, I can picture my wise mother always emphasizing the importance of how we present ourselves at work. Ever since the end of slavery and the Civil Rights movement, Black people have always focused on working twice as hard and twice as well as their white counterparts, who only needed to have a third of the skills. So, I took her advice to heart — dress professionally and always look corporately presentable. In my eyes, I was thin, but white America had a different viewpoint. To fit in, my skirts needed to be longer and slightly looser — all to ensure my curves were not a distraction. Not just to white men, mind you, but to white women who might envy the God-given curves they wish they had.

Despite my efforts and the positive feedback pouring in from various corners of the corporate world, it was not smooth sailing. My supervisors felt my skirts were too tight and too high. Confused, I would double-check with my mom; we would scrutinize my wardrobe together, ensuring my skirts always hit the knees and not a centimeter higher. I began to realize being black and professional was not two words accepted in the same sentence. I found myself crying, holding my chest as if I were about to have a heart attack. I wanted to quit, put my degree in the drawer, and stay home. Why must I fight a fight I did not start?

I must say it was exhausting, always having to worry about how my income was attached to the size of my ass. Really? The struggle to be seen for your skills and not just your appearance, all while grappling with the conflicting standards imposed by the corporate world. And do you know what? I excelled at my job — punctual, effective, creative, and an advocate for our clients. But for my supervisors, it was not enough. They were fixated on my appearance, critiquing the very fabric of my being. It was a journey filled with panic attacks and sometimes suicidal thoughts because I began to believe I did not belong. It has been over 20 years since I wore a skirt to work. I still have a fear of being criticized about my shape and whether my God-given curves would be offensive to the majority.

## ROLL YOUR TONGUE

Let us chat about something close to home for many of you, including myself — the constant mispronunciation of names. This universal microaggression sneaks into the corporate landscape, affecting individuals of diverse backgrounds, especially professionals of color. And let me tell you, it is more than just an innocent mistake; it reflects a deeper issue of acceptance and respect for cultural differences.

Wendy Flenoury was the name my father gave my big sister, and she, in turn, passed it on to me. I was always told it was a pretty and "easygoing name." Easy going? What did that mean? I never felt comfortable with that comment, but I was always told that in school. I am not going to discuss how I was always mistaken for a little white female before I even showed up. Here comes the constant mispronunciation of my last name: "So Miss Flanry" or "Flnory." WOW! The "u" is the only silent letter. So, for years, white people never said my last name correctly because it was not easy to articulate.

The constant mispronunciation of names, often from a lack of effort or genuine interest, creates an environment where individuals of diverse backgrounds, particularly professionals of color, grapple with a sense of frustration and invisibility.

"Thanks, Dad, for naming my sister and me after a white woman you had a crush on."

\*\*\*

Imagine you walk into the office daily, and your name, something so inherently personal, is consistently mispronounced.

It is not just a misstep; it is a subtle message that your cultural heritage does not matter, and your identity is not worthy of acknowledgment. Names carry profound cultural significance and are integral to one's identity. [1] This microaggression is a characteristic of a broader issue within the workplace: a failure to embrace and respect the diverse backgrounds that contribute to the richness of the corporate tapestry. The article "The Racist Practice of Mispronouncing" reported that "having an uncommon name can cause anxiety and alienation."[2]

Remember during the presidential race, Fox News TV's Tucker Carlson, in his angry rant, then Georgia's Senator David Perdue's remark to Trump's supporters, continuously mispronounced Joe Biden's running mate, Kamala Harris' name. Richard Goodstein stated that Carlson dismissively responded, "OK. So what?" Retorting to Carlson's response, Goodstein replied, "I think out of respect for someone who is going to be on the national ticket, pronouncing her name right is a bare minimum."[3]

The constant exposure to microaggressions and the subsequent deployment of the shield of intent can contribute to feelings of isolation, imposter syndrome, and a heightened awareness of their racial identity.[4] The workplace, which should ideally be a space for professional growth, becomes a battleground for navigating subtle yet impactful acts of racism. Mispronouncing names is not merely a matter of linguistic correctness but a dismissal of the cultural significance of names.

---

[1] Hall, Stuart. "Cultural Identity and Diaspora." In Colonial discourse and post-colonial theory, pp. 392-403. Routledge, 2015.
[2] Alicia Noreiga, "Facilitating Black Identity and Advocacy: Creating Cellphones for Reflecting on Issues Affecting Black Students," Visual Studies 37, no. 1-2 (2022): 11–21.
[3] Baker, Sinead Tucker Carlson was furious after a guest corrected his pronunciation of Kamala Harris' name. Business Insider 2020.
[4] Jarldorn, Michele, and Kathomi Gatwiri. "Shaking off the imposter syndrome: Our place in the resistance." In The Palgrave handbook of imposter syndrome in higher education, pp. 529-543. Cham: Springer International Publishing, 2022.

For professionals of color, whose names often carry deep roots in their heritage,[1] the consistent mispronunciation can be more than an inconvenience. It becomes a daily reminder that their identity is not fully acknowledged or respected within the corporate environment. This subtle disregard creates a profound sense of alienation as professionals of color navigate a professional landscape where their cultural nuances are overlooked.

## IMPACT OF MISPRONUNCIATION

This microaggression can hinder effective communication and collaboration within the workplace. When names are consistently mispronounced, it becomes a barrier to building authentic relationships and establishing trust among co-workers. The lack of effort to master the correct pronunciation can perpetuate a culture where diversity is superficially acknowledged but not genuinely embraced.

"That was not my intent" becomes a powerful tool to perpetuate these microaggressions. It allows individuals to distance themselves from the impact of their actions, creating a disconnect between intention and effect. The comment by Tucker Carlson, "OK, so what," is a form of deleting accountability and minimizing his intended disrespect and racism toward VP Mrs. Harris.

For the individuals offering these microaggressions, the shield of intent may provide a false sense of innocence, allowing them to maintain a positive self-image despite perpetuating harmful behaviors. A meta-analysis review by Pieterse et al. [2] found an 86% correlation between experiences of racism and mental distress — in particular, depression and anxiety.

---

[1] Wilentz, Gay. "Civilizations Underneath: African Heritage as Cultural Discourse in Toni Morrison's Song of Solomon." In Toni Morrison's Fiction, pp. 109-133. Routledge, 2016.
[2] Pieterse, Alex L., Nathan R. Todd, Helen A. Neville, and Robert T. Carter. "Perceived racism and mental health among Black American adults: a meta-analytic review." Journal of counseling psychology 59, no. 1 (2012): 1.

I do not know about you, but it is exhausting and irritating to consistently correct folks at work on the pronunciation of your name. I understand that names require practice and the roll of the tongue, but every single time we see each other passing the coffee bar! The awkward moments of correcting mispronunciations are frequently a part of how professionals of color navigate the professional world. The burden frequently falls on the individual to update their co-workers, adding a layer of stress, uncertainty, and discomfort to their daily interactions.

## Ass-u-med: "Ass Out of You, Not Me."

After getting my master's degree in social work from the University of Southern California, I felt ready for the next level in my career. I applied for various jobs. However, I stepped out on faith and applied for a job with the government. I knew that by working for the government, I would have a steady income, great health insurance, and I could retire comfortably. Nevertheless, I did not know that applying for this job was going to land me in a physical fight with my white co-worker. This co-worker always had something derogatory, discriminatory, or racially motivated to say whenever she was in my presence. I knew she struggled with the fact that I was her immediate supervisor. I also knew that, with my youthful looks and soft voice, she assumed I was too young to have the position. What can I say? Black doesn't fade!

After working in that position for over a year and finally gaining the trust of my co-workers and my superiors, I knew I had found my safe space. I began to make six figures after being placed in a leadership position. I couldn't ignore the reality that a good number of my non-Black co-workers were constantly trying to make me appear incompetent. One year, at a department Christmas lunch, everyone had gathered to celebrate the holidays. As we were standing in line getting food, my white coworker approached me and asked me if my hair was real. Before I could say anything, she reached up with her left hand, grasped the back of my hair, and yanked it. I stumbled and almost dropped my plate of food. I immediately felt anger rise in my chest and shoot into my fist. I WAS HEATED! My acquaintance grasped my wrist just as I raised my arm to strike her in the rear end. I bet you she will never make that assumption again.

It was at that moment that I realized I had blacked out and was ready to risk it all. I was prepared to go to jail for beating her ass. How dare she think it was her right to question anything on my body and touch me? She touched my hair! Anyone who knows anything about Black women should not put their hands in their hair. And trust me, whether we grew it out of our heads or bought it, it is ours! This stereotype suggests that only certain bone-straight hair types are considered "normal" or "acceptable," and that textured or coiled hair is considered to contribute to biases and discrimination. Can you believe all she got was a write-up from my superior? If it were the other way around, I would have been fired and charged with assault.

Black professionals often contend with preconceived notions that can be limiting and frustrating. The assumption that they all share the same cultural background neglects the reality of the diverse heritage within the Black community, which encompasses a myriad of ethnicities, nationalities, and traditions. This oversimplification perpetuates stereotypes and undermines the individuality of Black leaders, hindering their ability to express their unique perspectives and contributions.

In the face of these challenges, Black leaders often confront a delicate balance between asserting their individuality and navigating the expectations thrust upon them. They must work doubly hard to dispel stereotypes and showcase the breadth of experiences that inform their leadership styles. This constant effort to challenge assumptions can be mentally and emotionally taxing, diverting energy that could be better invested in driving innovation and fostering inclusive workplaces.

The experiences of professionals of color in the complex landscape of corporate America have often been marred by the subtle yet insidious phenomenon known as "selective amnesia microaggression."[1] This form of discrimination manifests when individuals conveniently forget or overlook the contributions of professionals of color during discussions or acknowledgments, perpetuating a cycle of omission that hinders progress toward diversity and inclusion. It is like a sly magician, making achievements disappear from the conversation.

Imagine you are in a meeting, giving your all, breaking through barriers, and reaching leadership heights. You are excited to finally get the opportunity to show what you can do for that big promotion you were working so hard for. But here is the twist: when it is time to acknowledge the efforts, your contributions are written in invisible ink.

Professionals of color in corporate settings frequently encounter challenges that stem from historical biases and systemic inequalities. Despite breaking through barriers to attain leadership roles, their achievements are sometimes marginalized or ignored. These microaggressions undermine their hard work, perpetuate harmful stereotypes, and reinforce an environment where recognition is unequal.

Historically, Black inventors have been routinely removed from history as significant contributors to various fields such as health care, technology, mental health, etc. Benjamin Banneker was an African American mathematician, astronomer, and inventor born in 1731.[2] He was the one who created the first wooden clock the United States has ever known. His work as an abolitionist was

---

[1] Alicia Noreiga (2022) Facilitating Black identity and advocacy: creating cellphones for reflecting on issues affecting Black students, Visual Studies, 37:1-2, 11–21, DOI:10.1080/1472586X.2022.2042371KUOW - The racist practice of mispronouncing names

[2] Morgan, Thaddeus. "8mBlack Inventors who made daily life easier." History.com. A&E Television Networks (2019). https://www.history.com/news/8-black-inventors-african-american

part of the idea of ending slavery. He corresponded with Thomas Jefferson to advocate against the mistreatment of Black people in America. Nevertheless, how many of us knew that?

Mary Van Brittan Brown, born in 1922, invented and patented a home security system in 1966. She was concerned about the high crime rate in her apartment building, so she created a security system that residents could monitor inside their homes. She also designed the remote-control locking system. Is her family getting royalties from all these companies utilizing their unique technology to care for their families and families worldwide?

## IMPACT OF OMISSION

The impact of selective amnesia microaggression is far-reaching. It creates a hostile work environment where professionals of color may feel undervalued, overlooked, and disheartened, hindering their career advancement. The lack of recognition also reinforces stereotypes about competence and leadership abilities, perpetuating a cycle of exclusion that makes it difficult for other Black professionals to ascend to leadership roles.

In the scene of the Tyler Perry show *Sistas*, the character Aaron is a light-skinned African American male from London who created a multi-million-dollar law firm company; however, he is not the face of the company. He informed his love interest, Andi, that he built this business and was so successful because his white partners were put on the face of the company so that people would take him seriously. It was a move that quite a few of us, me included, have contemplated when building our business. It is the belief that if you do business with white people, your business will be seen as valued, and you will be taken seriously. However, if you are seen as a Black business, then your business is not worthy of their attention or support.

The omission of Black professionals from discussions about company achievements, milestones, or successes isolates the next generation of Black professionals from learning from the past. In boardrooms and meetings, the contributions of Black executives may be downplayed or overlooked, contributing to a pervasive narrative that fails to acknowledge the diversity of talent and expertise within the organization.

## WE ARE NOT ALL THE SAME

Stereotyping microaggressions is the subtle assignment of tasks rooted in racial preconceptions. Individuals are often grouped into projects or roles based on preconceived notions about their abilities, skills, or work style. For instance, Black leaders might find themselves disproportionately assigned to diversity and inclusion initiatives or roles that involve public-facing tasks, reinforcing the stereotype that they are better suited for such responsibilities.

One significant challenge faced by Black leaders is the existence of harmful stereotypes that can hinder their progress within corporate settings. Stereotypes rooted in racial bias can cast shadows over the achievements and qualifications of black professionals, leading to unwarranted doubts about their capabilities. This can create a hostile environment where Black leaders must continually prove their competence, facing the burden of dispelling preconceived notions based on their racial identity.

These stereotypes, in turn, contribute to the limitation of professional growth opportunities for Black leaders. Despite their qualifications and accomplishments, they may be included in critical decision-making circles or overlooked for high-profile assignments.

During the George Floyd murder in 2020, there was a mass hiring wave of black professionals in the positions of diversity, equity, and inclusion (DEI).[1] Why? Corporate America wanted to show that they supported having people of color in high-powered positions, but only in positions where they felt they

---

[1] Bray Jr, Charles Edward. "Diversity, Equity, and Inclusion Post George Floyd and COVID-19: Reflections from Global Business Leaders on a Changing Paradigm." PhD diss., Pepperdine University, 2023.

looked good through the minority's lens. Their "intent" was to appear to look inclusive and to show sensitivity to people of color who had been fighting for the rights of equality for centuries. However, the "intent" was only to cover up the underlying foundation of continued racism to control how black professionals were seen in higher positions.

Despite these challenges, professionals of color in corporate America continue to break barriers and pave the way for change. Our resilience, determination, and ability to overcome systemic obstacles stand as a testament to the strength of individuality.

## CRUISIN' IN SAFE SPACES

Creating safe spaces for Black leaders in corporate America involves initiative-taking measures that address microaggressions and promote a culture of inclusion. By raising awareness, establishing clear policies, encouraging open communication, providing mentorship, celebrating diversity, conducting regular audits, and empowering allies, organizations can contribute to a workplace where Black leaders can thrive without the pervasive impact of subtle discrimination. Taking proactive steps to address these issues and cultivate a workplace where individuals can thrive is crucial.

Here are six comprehensive tips for navigating microaggressions and creating safe spaces within the professional realm.

- **Promote Awareness and Education:** Encourage ongoing education on microaggressions and their impact. Conduct training sessions that help employees recognize and understand these subtle forms of discrimination. By fostering awareness, individuals can be more mindful of their behaviors and work collectively to eliminate microaggressions.
- **Encourage Open Communication:** Foster a culture of open communication where employees feel

comfortable discussing their experiences and concerns. Establish channels, such as anonymous reporting systems, for employees to report microaggressions without fear of retaliation. By encouraging dialogue, organizations can address issues promptly and effectively.

- **Provide Mentorship and Sponsorship Programs:** Implement mentorship and sponsorship programs that connect Black leaders with experienced mentors or sponsors within the organization. These relationships offer support, guidance, and advocacy, helping them navigate challenges and advance in their careers.
- **Celebrate Diversity and Inclusion:** Creating a positive narrative around diversity reinforces the value of different perspectives and fosters a sense of belonging for all employees.
- **Conduct Regular Diversity Audits:** Periodically assess the workplace environment through diversity audits to identify any patterns of microaggressions or systemic issues. Use the findings to adjust policies, procedures, and training programs. Regular audits demonstrate a commitment to continuous improvement in fostering a safe and inclusive workplace.
- **Empower Allies and Advocates:** Encourage the development of allyship and advocacy programs that engage employees in actively supporting their Black co-workers. Allies can play a pivotal role in challenging microaggressions, fostering a culture of inclusion, and amplifying the voices of underrepresented leaders.

Raising awareness is the first step. Let us ensure everyone in the office knows what microaggressions are and why they are a big deal. But talking is not enough; let us put some muscle behind those words. Clear policies that say, "Hey, we don't do discrimination here," can be a significant change.

## CONCLUSION

An office that encourages open communication is like a breath of fresh air. It is a safe space to voice their concerns, share experiences, and find common ground. Add a dash of mentorship to the mix, and you have a recipe for success. Providing guidance and support can make a world of difference. And what about chatting? An office that encourages open communication is like a breath of fresh air. Finally, allies—the unsung heroes. Empowering allies within the organization is like building an army against subtle discrimination. When we stand together, we stand stronger. So, let us roll up our sleeves, put our heads together, and make Corporate America a place where Black leaders do not just survive but truly thrive.

---

**Dr. Wendy Talley, DSW, LCSW**
https://drwendytalley.com
Dr. Wendy Talley is an internationally recognized corporate wellness expert and CEO helping large organizations improve culture by training leaders as EQ experts. With 23 years of experience providing EAP services, staff development, and coaching, she's a sought-after keynote speaker and consultant who's worked with diverse leaders to promote workplace mental health and well-being.

# 13

# THE CORPORATE MAZE
## Roadblocks and Broken Ladders

JUDY ELLIS

*Not everything that is faced can be changed, but nothing can be changed until it is faced.*

—James Baldwin

Picture yourself stepping into a gleaming corporate lobby. Polished, marble floors stretch below your feet, promising a clear path to success. But beneath the surface, a labyrinth of hidden barriers awaits. Walls of implicit bias twist and turn, dead ends of microaggression block your way, and the subtle sting of unfair treatment hangs heavy in the air. This seductive façade promises a level playing field where talent and results alone determine success. As Sharla Horton-Williams points out in her chapter, the illusion of an employee experience, where every employee can navigate their career path on equal footing, trips up Black professionals and organizational engagement efforts to help Black employees. In the corporate maze, success isn't just about competence and outcomes, but about navigating roadblocks and deciphering cryptic clues, often woven from the impact of systemic bias.

Despite talent and qualifications, Black professionals consistently occupy the bottom rungs of corporate ladders in hiring [1], performance ratings [2], promotion, representation, pay equity, [3] retention, and employee engagement [4]. According to McKinsey & Company's 2021 report, *Race in the Workplace: The Black Experience in the US Private Sector*, "on the current trajectory, it will take about 95 years for Black employees to reach talent parity (or 12 percent representation) across all levels in the private sector." [5] Consider the fact that Black women are now the most educated group in the U.S., according to research from the National Center for Education Statistics [6]. Yet "they represent just 8 percent of private sector jobs and hold less than 2 percent of leadership positions." [7] Additionally, projections from the National

[1] Quillian, Lincoln, Ole Hexel, Arnfinn Midtboen, and Devah Pager. "Hiring Discrimination against Black Americans Hasn't Declined in 25 Years." Harvard Business Review, October 11, 2017. https://hbr.org/2017/10/hiring-discrimination-against-black-americans-hasnt-declined-in-25-years.

[2] Alba, Davey, et al. "Racial Disparities in Performance Evaluations at The New York Times." 2022 Report on Racial Disparities in Performance Evaluations, August 23, 2022. https://www.nyguild.org/2022-nyt-performance-evaluations-report.

[3] Lang, Kevin, and Jee-Yeon K. Lehmann. "Racial Discrimination in the Labor Market: Theory and Empirics." Journal of Economic Literature 50, no. 4 (2012): 959–1006. http://www.jstor.org/stable/23644909.

[4] Field, Emily, Alexis Krivkovich, Sandra Kugele, Nicole Robinson, and Lareina Yee. "Women in the Workplace 2023." McKinsey & Company, October 5, 2023. https://www.mckinsey.com/featured-insights/diversity-and-inclusion/women-in-the-workplace.

[5] Hancock, Brian, James Manyika, Lareina Yee, and Jackie Wong. "Race in the Workplace: The Black Experience in the US Private Sector." McKinsey & Company, February 21, 2021. https://www.mckinsey.com/featured-insights/diversity-and-inclusion/race-in-the-workplace-the-black-experience-in-the-us-private-sector.

[6] "Https://Nces.Ed.Gov/Fastfacts/Display.Asp?Id=72." Fast Facts, National Center for Education Statistics, August 2023. https://nces.ed.gov/fastfacts/display.asp?id=72.

[7] Helm, Angela Bronner. "Black Women Now the Most Educated Group in the US." The Root, June 5, 2016. https://www.theroot.com/black-women-now-the-most-educated-group-in-us-1790855540.

Committee on Pay Equity indicate that Black women may not achieve pay parity until 2059[1].

While the struggles of marginalized groups often share common roots, the Black professional's journey in the corporate maze takes on a distinct form, a chronic cough in a world catching a sniffle. Examining the challenges Black professionals face in corporate life is not just about acknowledging their individual struggles, but about illuminating the systemic biases that ultimately hinder everyone. By dismantling the barriers that disproportionately impact Black employees, we unleash a wellspring of diverse perspectives and drive better outcomes for all.

Prior to serving in my current role as a global Diversity, Equity, and Inclusion (DEI) consulting practice leader, my career unfolded in two distinct chapters: navigating the intricacies of a Fortune 50 company for a decade and over twenty years of building my expertise as the owner of two DEI consultancies. Drawing on the lessons learned from both worlds, this chapter sheds light on the less obvious, systemic hindrances that can limit the success and well-being of Black professionals. I share real-life examples and offer practical strategies that both organizations and individuals can implement to create more equitable and empowering environments.

## MY PERSONAL JOURNEY

*You can read a thousand books about war, but you'll never truly understand it until you hear the first gunshot.*

—Phil Caputo

While an undergraduate student at Indiana University, I was thrilled to win a fellowship to delve into a topic of my choice.

---

[1] "National Committee on Pay Equity." PayEquity.Org, January 1, 1970. https://www.pay-equity.org/#:~:text=African%20American%20women%20are%20not,see%20equal%20pay%20until%202059.

I wanted to explore "The Challenges of Black Managers in Corporate America," based on narratives shared by my older sisters' friends, who were 10-15 years my senior and Black pioneers in roles that encompassed engineering, corporate law, health care management, and media. Despite their high-level achievements, they each recounted personal experiences ranging from isolation to outright harassment. Intrigued, I presented this as my chosen topic to my fellowship advisor, a department chair at the Kelley School of Business. To my surprise, he asserted, "That's not an issue–I've never heard or read about it." He then challenged me to conduct an exhaustive search of existing literature.

In the pre-internet era, this proved a daunting task. I unearthed only one article and two books, only one accessible through inter-library processes: *The Black Manager: Making it in the Corporate World* by Floyd and Jacqueline Dickens, published in 1982.[1] The work, stemming from Jacqueline's master's in social work thesis research and Floyd's corporate experience, introduced a four-phased developmental model focused on self-development and coping strategies for Black managers entering predominantly White institutions. Armed with this research, my advisor was persuaded that the issue warranted further exploration.

Throughout that summer, I conducted numerous interviews with Black corporate professionals and their accounts painted a disheartening picture. My mother, a high school English teacher, and my father, an electrician, traveled to attend my final fellowship presentation. They were each taken aback by the audacity of my chosen topic. Having experienced bias in their respective educational journeys, they expressed disbelief that such research was even permitted at a predominantly White university. After my presentation, my parents commented that they weren't sure why I wanted to work in business after all I'd found out. Being young and green at the time, I failed to see the

---

[1] Dickens, Floyd, and Jacqueline B. Dickens. The Black Manager: Making it in the Corporate World. New York, NY: Amacom, 1982.

connection. However, the interview process for my first corporate role was about to teach me an extremely difficult lesson.

Near the end of my time at Indiana University, I stood at the entrance to the corporate maze, clutching an invitation to a recruiting event weekend at the headquarters of a consumer goods powerhouse. After successfully completing my on-campus interview, the invite seemed like the promise of a smooth path to the middle class. My college campus was within 150 miles of the corporate headquarters and what felt like the gateway into my professional journey, yet I lacked two crucial tools: a car and a major credit card. The recruiter assured me that rental cars could be covered for students with financial limitations. But as I approached the Hertz desk, the maze unveiled its first hidden wall.

The attendant, scrutinizing me like a gatekeeper, demanded a major credit card, ignoring the "No credit card required" that was clearly highlighted beside my name on the reservation. "Big wigs in Cincinnati promised you what?" he scoffed, snatching the reservation printout away from my view. "I'm in charge here, and you don't get a car without a credit card."

Astounded, I called Hertz corporate from a nearby payphone. The agent confirmed my reservation was credit-card-free, then called the local agent on another line while I was on hold. I heard the agent tell them, "Black girl, no credit card, no car!" before he hung up. My blood ran cold. This wasn't a simple misunderstanding; it was blatant bias.

Hertz promised to escalate the issue to the franchise owner. But what was left of my hope dissolved when I saw the local agent lock the phone away in his desk and stroll out of the facility. My frustration simmered with each step he took. It felt like he was carrying my entire future away with him. My pathway to what I perceived as a new, independent life was crumbling because of this person's prejudiced behavior.

Cathy, my unwavering friend who had driven me to the airport offered to use her credit card for the rental, but by then, I was running late for the opening dinner. I called the recruiter, bracing for more disappointment. To my surprise, he voiced disgust with the actions of the agent and urged me to come no matter the delay. When the local agent finally reappeared, Cathy and I walked to his desk and offered her credit card, hearts heavy but heads held high. He rudely shoved the paperwork through the window, along with the keys for a car – one I later found was woefully lacking oil and washer fluid. Though the rental car ordeal caused me to arrive near the end of the first evening's dinner, I did what so many Black professionals do when we overcome these hurdles. I put on a smile and downplayed the impact of the incident because I didn't want to draw negative attention to myself. I ultimately received a job offer, but the experience left a painful impression that stays with me to this day.

## Leadership Lessons

- Recognize the Potential for Bias: My car rental journey reveals the insidious nature of bias that can impede seemingly neutral processes. Awareness is the first step in dismantling these obstacles.
- Address Financial Hurdles: Requiring socially disadvantaged candidates to navigate financial hurdles for an interview can create inequity in your hiring processes. To foster fairness, organizations should consider proactively eliminating such barriers by prepaying expenses for candidates.
- Train Recruiters: Provide recruiters with education to not only recognize systemic issues but actively probe candidates' needs to achieve true inclusivity in the hiring process.

## Unwelcomed Arrival

Before Sharilyn, a Black executive, began her first day with a professional services company, she and her husband embarked on a cross-country move. Amidst the excitement of relocating to a new community, her optimism collided with an unexpected and disheartening encounter with a new neighbor. When the moving truck arrived, due to the short distance between Sharilyn's and a neighbor's driveways, the truck partially blocked the neighbor's driveway, but still allowed enough space for a car to get in or out. As Sharilyn's husband removed items from the truck, the neighbor ran outside and began yelling about being "blocked inside" her home. Instead of inquiring about how long the truck would be there, she demanded that he move it, not only from in front of her house, but off the entire street immediately and threatened to involve the police.

Not stopping there, the neighbor further escalated the situation by calling him the n-word, before calling the police. Upon arrival, the police questioned the validity of the neighbor's distress, stating, "Your driveway isn't even totally blocked." Sharilyn ended a virtual business meeting early to go outside and support her husband. Thankfully, the police de-escalated the situation and placed blame on the neighbor, who continuously screamed the racial epithet.

Despite having dealt with this extremely stressful and potentially dangerous situation, Sharilyn had to continue the professional responsibilities of her day. She went back inside and continued her virtual meetings, having to push aside the anger, disappointment, and trauma that she and her husband had just experienced.

LEADERSHIP LESSONS

- Transparency and Open Communication: Encourage managers to create a safe space for employees to voice concerns and advocate for their needs regarding obstacles encountered during transitions.
- Resource Preparation: Be prepared with resources (e.g., mental health support, and cultural awareness training) for managers to address relocation-related cultural problems.

- Flexibility: Be prepared to adjust timelines and expectations to better support employees grappling with race-related difficulties.

## THE MERITOCRACY MYTH

*The function, the very serious function of racism is a distraction. It keeps you from doing your work. It keeps you explaining, over and over again, your reason for being.*

—Toni Morrison

Researchers investigated human resource data from 2014 to 2020, analyzing 9,037 employees within a prominent professional services firm [1]. Their primary focus was on the influence of co-workers' racial composition on turnover and promotion among employees. Notably, Black women emerged as the only group with turnover and promotion rates distinctly affected by the racial identity of their co-workers.[2]

The study revealed that a 14-percentage point increase in the proportion of White co-workers correlated with a significant 10.6 percentage point rise in turnover specifically for Black women. This effect, however, was not observed for other employees of color, including similarly sized numerical minorities such as Black men or Hispanic women and men.[3] Black women reported various ways in which interactions with majority White co-workers negatively impacted their participation. Challenges were described related to task assignments and performance evaluations, potentially leading to Black women being labeled as

---

[1] Linos, Elizabeth, Sanaz Mobassari, and Nina Roussille. "Asymmetric Peer Effects at Work: The Effect of White Coworkers on Black Women's Careers." Harvard Kennedy School, November 1, 2023. https://www.hks. harvard.edu/publications/asymmetric-peer-effects-work-effect-white-coworkers-black-womens-careers.
[2] Linos, "Asymmetric Peer Effects at Work."
[3] Linos, "Asymmetric Peer Effects at Work."

low performers, which contributed to increased turnover over time.[1]

Disturbingly, Black women are "nearly two and a half times more likely than white women — and over three times more likely than men — to encounter surprise about their language skills or other abilities."[2] While individual microaggressions may seem insignificant, their cumulative impact, occurring day after day, takes a toll on well-being and professional engagement, driving a constant need to over-perform, validate, and double-check. The meritocracy myth, that pristine level playing field where talent reigns supreme, starts to show its cracks, revealing a landscape rife with systemic hurdles and implicit biases.

## PROVE IT AGAIN BIAS

*It's not the load that breaks you down, it's the way you carry it.*

—Lena Horne

Working in the consulting trenches exposed me to difficult organizational realities, but few resonate as deeply as the insidious nature of Prove It Again bias. Research by the American Bar Association and LeanIn.org confirms what so many Black professionals intuitively know: a persistent demand exists for additional evidence to prove themselves, which tilts the playing field in the supposed meritocracy. In fact, according to the study, women of color reported higher levels of Prove It Again bias than any other group—35 percentage points higher than White men.[3] Because Black women's judgment is more likely to be questioned,

---

[1] Linos, "Asymmetric Peer Effects at Work."

[2] "The State of Black Women in Corporate America." Lean In, 2020. https://leanin.org/research/state-of-black-women-in-corporate-america/introduction.

[3] Williams, Joan. "You Can't Change What You Can't See." American Bar Association's Commission on Women in the Profession and the Minority Corporate Counsel Association, (2018). https://www.americanbar.org/content/dam/aba/administrative/women/you-cant-change-what-you-cant-see-print.pdf.

they often face requests for additional evidence of their competence.

Twenty-five years ago, as a novice financial analyst at a Fortune 50 global consumer products company, I managed fabric care marketing budgets for well-known laundry brands, but a persistent challenge emerged when a brand seemed to be hemorrhaging cash beyond its allocated budget. During monthly meetings with the brand manager, I observed that though he spoke confidently, he offered flimsy stories to support his numbers. Upon expressing my concerns to my manager, Mike, I received a dismissive response, where he asserted his confidence in the brand manager and told me not to worry. Despite presenting meticulous reports as evidence of my assertions, my input was summarily dismissed with a curt, "Not an issue."

By the third month, the financial shortfall reached a million dollars, intensifying my anxiety. I faced belittlement from Mike in front of the team whenever I brought it up. I was publicly humiliated when he angrily said, "Judy, you don't know what happens over the course of several months on these budgets. I've told you before that you are mistaken!" His only consolation came in the form of a box of tissues that he pushed across his desk towards me as a tear escaped from my eye and rolled down my cheek. It was not only the embarrassment that brought me to tears, but it was also the fear that, when it all came out in the open, the blame would fall on me.

Feeling desperate, I bypassed Mike and a strict company protocol by taking my concerns to Veronica, our Associate Director. Even after I presented her with the data and blunt facts, Veronica exhibited skepticism about my concerns. She immediately launched into the textbook refrain of "I've known Dan for years, he wouldn't..." I watched the report disappear into her drawer, along with my hope of being heard. I had spent hours reworking and rechecking the accuracy of my findings, and it felt demoralizing to have my work repeatedly disregarded.

After a month of fear for my job and personal anguish over my treatment, an unexpected shift occurred when Veronica suddenly called me into her office. Walking in, I saw my report sitting open on her desk. In the subsequent conversation, which was devoid of emotion or acknowledgment of my work, she explained that the brand manager's financial misconduct had been exposed and he was no longer at the company. Then she abruptly ended the meeting. While I was incredibly relieved to have the issue finally resolved, I was also deeply disappointed. As I walked out of her office, I looked towards Mike, who also never apologized or even acknowledged that I uncovered the issue. Their Prove It Again bias had severely impacted my personal well-being and employee experience, contributing to my thoughts of leaving the company.

## LEADERSHIP LESSONS

- Question Data, Trust Evidence: Encourage a culture where data is rigorously questioned, and decisions are grounded in objective evidence rather than assumptions or personal opinions.
- Challenge Biases: Actively promote an environment where biases are identified and challenged. Be vigilant about recognizing and addressing biases, fostering inclusivity.
- Foster Open Communication: Create a space where team members feel comfortable voicing concerns without fear of retribution. Establish mechanisms for employees to speak up with assurance that their concerns will be taken seriously.

## PERFORMANCE BIAS

The concept of merit-based advancement is a foundational principle in many workplaces. However, research reveals a contrasting reality, exposing persistent biases that can distort performance evaluations and undermine this principle. A 2022 Textio study, analyzing language in performance feedback, scrutinized over 25,000 written reviews and surveyed 500 employees. The findings showed that individuals from marginalized groups received more personality-based feedback and less concrete, actionable input on the quality of their work. Notably, 100% of Black and Latinx individuals reported receiving personality feedback.[1]

Furthermore, a Harvard Business Review article emphasizes the tendency of "raters to lowball women and minorities" in performance reviews.[2] In a collaboration with a law firm to audit their performance evaluations, significant disparities emerged, particularly along lines of race and gender. Only "9.5% of individuals from diverse backgrounds received mentions of leadership in their performance evaluations," representing a shortfall of over 70 percentage points compared to evaluations for White women in the same context.[3]

Towards the end of my decade in corporate America, amid the era of exorbitant copy machine use, I worked alone one evening. While making copies, I stumbled upon Cindy's performance review, written by our mutual manager, and her associated feedback from colleagues and customers. The peer and customer feedback had a consistent theme regarding the need for enhanced competency and reliability, essential qualities in our advisory position. Despite this, our manager's portrayal presented her as a "water walker" who was exceptionally competent and fostered enduring customer confidence. Not true.

In contrast, my review, despite overwhelmingly positive customer feedback, had a mediocre summary crafted by our manager, unfairly tinting the summary of my customer feedback and the overall tone of my evaluation. Despite not seeing my final rating, I knew this was not the caliber of performance review that I had been accustomed to receiving.

[1] "Job Performance Feedback Is Heavily Biased." Textio.com, June 15, 2022. https://textio.com/blog/job-performance-feedback-is-heavily-biased-new-textio-report/75983880330.
[2] Dobbin, Frank, and Alexandra Kalev. "Why Diversity Programs Fail." Harvard Business Review, 2016. https://hbr.org/2016/07/why-diversity-programs-fail.
[3] Dobbin. "Why Diversity Programs Fail."

Armed with what I perceived as a smoking gun, I sought guidance from a vice president whom I considered a mentor. He acknowledged that Cindy's review had been unjustly inflated while mine had been unfairly understated. He told me, "You deserve much better than this." Yet his response, reflecting the harsh realities of the corporate maze, was cautionary. He discouraged HR involvement, citing potential backlash that could impede "real future opportunities for advancement." He instead pledged that he would "try to advocate for" me in an upcoming performance rating discussion. It didn't sound promising.

Despite my disheartenment, I attempted to advocate for myself during my review. That prompted a meeting with the executive leading our area where they made every attempt to gaslight me into believing that the inaccurate review was somehow "really good." This response only further deepened the corporate labyrinth for me.

Ultimately, recognizing the delicate balance of the tightrope I walked, I chose not to pursue further action. While disheartened by the lack of active advocacy, I navigated the maze, understanding that unveiling this type of systemic bias was a crucial step in advocating for transparency and accountability. In hindsight, I now see this as a turning point in my career journey, fueling my passion to work full-time in creating more equitable organizational processes.

## LEADERSHIP LESSONS

Awareness is power. The first step in dismantling bias is recognizing it, both in yourself and others. Educate yourself and advocate for transparency in evaluation processes, fostering a culture of authenticity.

Analyze systems. The American Bar Association's *Interrupting Racial & Gender Bias in the Legal Profession* report[1] suggests a two-pronged approach that starts with de-biasing structural processes and systems, then addressing the biased behaviors of individuals by raising awareness, acknowledging right behaviors, and ensuring accountability for wrong ones.

Separate personality issues from skill sets to appraise each apart from the other. Women and people of color are typically allowed a much smaller range of acceptable behaviors than White men. For example, women may be labeled "aggressive" for the same behaviors that are widely acceptable in men.

## FINAL THOUGHTS

*Happiness comes from living as you need to, as you want to. As your inner voice tells you to. Happiness comes from being who you actually are instead of who you think you are supposed to be.*
—Shonda Rhimes

As a Black professional in the corporate workplace, don't plan on your success looking exactly like that of your counterparts. Hidden barriers, both inside and outside of the workplace, can take your journey in directions you never expected. Listen to yourself and keep your *eyes wide open*. Be intentional about your career and choose what works for you. Embrace your distinctness and recognize your effort also paves the way for a more equitable and inclusive landscape for others.

The African proverb, "If you want to go fast, go alone. If you want to go far, go together," contains cultural wisdom that speaks directly to your professional journey. Seek out a community of trusted allies who grasp the intricate terrain of your

---

[1] Williams, Joan C., Marina Multhaup, Su Li, and Rachel Korn "You Can't Change What You Can't See." American Bar Association and ABA Commission on Women in the Profession. 2018
https://www.americanbar.org/content/dam/aba/administrative/women/you-cant-change-what-you-cant-see-print.pdf

chosen path. Their support will not only refine your individual skills but also serve as a reminder of your inherent worth. Remember, external validation is fleeting; true success resonates from forging your own path, empowered by the strength of those who believe in you and your vision. Shift focus away from a frantic ascent of the broken corporate ladder - it's not the sole route to fulfillment. Achievement isn't determined by conforming to the rigid expectations set by others but by breaking free and crafting a future true to yourself.

## Judy Ellis

As SVP and Head of DEI Advisory for global HR services company AMS, Judy Ellis designs talent and culture solutions while coaching leaders on growing inclusive teams where employees thrive, innovate, and deliver results. She leverages Fortune 50 expertise and 20+ years of consulting to listen deeply, find data-driven solutions, inspire unity, and accelerate progress.

# 14

# INVISIBLE LEADERSHIP

## Ansar Saalih

I felt the mood shift as soon as the words left my mouth, "Yes sir. I am a Muslim." My commander's eyes narrowed for just a moment before he caught himself and nodded. In that instance, I knew that I would be considered an outsider.

I was already the only Black male officer in the room. And now, I was exposed. My commander was a devout Christian and member of the Church of Latter-Day Saints. In the military, service members can discuss religion provided one was not attempting to convert. And my commander, who was proud of his Christianity, openly discussed religion, which was fine. But The Department of Defense prohibits unlawful discrimination of any kind, including religious discrimination.[1] But I already knew that's what the good ole Christian boy from Mississippi had in store for me.

Throughout my service in the Air Force, I overheard "locker room talk" from officers suspicious of Black Muslims. They made assumptions that we were affiliated with the Nation of Islam

---

[1] "Protections Against Discrimination and Other Prohibited Practices." 2021. Federal Trade Commission. November 24, 2021. https://www.ftc.gov/policy-notices/no-fear-act/protections-against-discrimination.

or a member of a sleeper cell. Had those stereotypes now affected how my commander saw me? Had I become a sleeper cell enemy in my commander's eyes? Or was it merely an unconscious bias against Muslims in general? Regardless of the reason, I could feel his perception shift like tectonic plates churning beneath my feet, destabilizing the ground on which I stood.

Most folks don't know – or want to know – that there are primarily two types of African American Muslims. What I've heard over the years is that in America, there is no difference. Muslim is Muslim. But there are differences, and those differences matter. There are members of the Nation of Islam (NOI) which was founded by Wallace D. Fard Muhammad in 1930 as an Islamic and Black nationalist movement. His mission was to educate the defenseless and downtrodden Black people about God and themselves.[1] But most African American Muslims today are Sunni Muslims who pray to Allah; there is Black Nationalist Movement. Although they are not members of the Nation of Islam, they follow the leadership of Imam Warith Deen Mohammed, the son of Elijah Muhammed.[2] Ironically, Elijah Muhammed led the Nation of Islam from 1932-1975.

What most white Americans don't know, and I suppose many African Americans too, is that Black Americans have been converting to Islam in significant numbers since the 1960s; many actually converted after reading *The Autobiography of Malcolm X*. The Black consciousness movement during that time sought to break free of the Christianity forced upon enslaved ancestors. And it makes sense. About 20% of Africans enslaved in North America were Muslims; conversion to them represented a return to their African spiritual roots.[3]

---

[1] "The Nation of Islam." 2021. National Archives. April 1, 2021.
https://www.archives.gov/research/african-americans/black-power/nation-of-islam.
[2] "This Far by Faith . 1967-TODAY: From CRISIS, A SEARCH FOR MEANING | PBS." n.d. https://www.pbs.org/thisfarbyfaith/journey_5/p_7.html.
[3] "This Far by Faith . 1967-TODAY: From CRISIS, A SEARCH FOR MEANING | PBS." n.d. https://www.pbs.org/thisfarbyfaith/journey_5/p_7.html.

Even if I educated my commander on military law and the history of Muslims in America, it wouldn't matter. And, there was no way I could have brought it up because he immediately distanced himself from me. Conversations became terse and guarded. My ideas were constantly questioned or attributed to others—behind closed doors and in front of others. I was given more administrative tasks, less autonomy, and was scrutinized and micromanaged for basic assignments. It was a subtle undermining—never overt discrimination—with a clear message that I was no longer a member of the inner circle.

## Losing Power, Choosing Influence

With my Commander closing doors, I faced a choice—challenge the system stacked against me or maneuver to influence it indirectly. Part of me wanted to call out the bias and microaggressions outright. But wisdom told me that playing the "race card" would only affirm stereotypes and make things even more difficult. I had seen it happen before — accusations of being the "angry Black man" were commonly used to undermine officers with legitimate grievances.

"Can you be yourself and still hide?" That was the question I kept asking myself. Because honestly, it was all bullsh*t. I clearly outshined the other flight commanders in leadership ability. Yet when my boss created obstacles where none existed, how was I able to properly lead? A Black Muslim in the Air Force, I knew I'd lose the war if I stood up to him head on, but I wasn't about to back down either. I ain't no punk. I had to resist without seeming combative. So, I bit my tongue, bided my time, and embraced invisible leadership as my strategy. I would fight this surreptitious war in my own way.

I started to funnel my ideas through my second-in-command, the Commander's rising star and top sounding board. I wasn't just going to use their relationship to my advantage, it was going to become an integral part of my strategy. My second-in-command quickly noticed the shift in my leadership style and went along with it. With part one of my plan activated, I focused my attention on helping my team adjust to the new dynamic; it wasn't long before they picked up on the change. I convinced them that everything was good and that I didn't need to be the Golden Boy or get credit for my ideas... I just wanted to see the results!

As Gerardo A. Dada states, "The best kind of leadership is invisible leadership, because it eliminates any trace of ego or self-centered interest that the leader may have and focuses on truly leading."[1] Leading this way focuses on creating positive change in people and organizations, not seeking personal power or credit. Many want power and position, but true leaders inspire by sharing an energizing vision of the future. They spark others to see the world through fresh eyes and to do things differently in order to make that vision a reality. Their passion and clarity of purpose earn followers independent of any formal authority. As Lao Tzu observed centuries ago, "A leader is best when people barely know he exists... When his aim is met, they will say, "We did it ourselves!"[2]

Even with the invisible leadership management style, my competence couldn't be denied although though credit was. Although I was shut out of meetings, I still influenced opinions, crafted strategies, and drafted long-term plans. My second-in-command presented every one of my ideas exactly how I laid it out, and he was showered with praise. My commander continued to believe that I was being punished but I was thriving the entire time. By implementing my ideas, the Golden Boy and I advanced our careers.

I continued to walk the tightrope of officership—contributing fully and delivering results while never seeming to

[1] Canaday, Sara. 2014. "True Leadership Is Invisible - Sara Canaday." *Acclaimed Leadership Strategist Sara Canaday* (blog). January 8, 2014.
[2] https://www.brainyquote.com/quotes/lao_tzu_121709

challenge the status quo. Technical expertise, strategic thinking, caring for the team—my qualifications outweighed all of their bigoted assumptions. My leadership was subterfuge, guiding invisibly because assumptions and prejudice blinded the commander to my voice. It was all good though. I had mastered influence and authority, caring for troops and country in ways no barrier could block. My true rank: concealed catalyst.

Dale Carnegie's How to Win Friends and Influence People gave me critical insights into leading through influence rather than authority. My "invisible leadership" relied wholly on bringing out the best in others through earnest empathy, feedback sans blame, and winsome guidance — all hallmarks of Carnegie's seminal work on interpersonal skill. As he wrote, the root of influence lies in "making the other person happy about doing the thing you suggest", and "A leader's job often includes changing your people's attitudes and behaviors," I took both to heart, internalizing his principles as guidelines to lead without formal authority.[1]

- Principle 1 – Begin with praise and honest appreciation.
- Principle 2 – Call attention to people's mistakes indirectly.
- Principle 3 – Talk about your own mistakes before criticizing others.
- Principle 4 – Ask questions instead of giving direct orders.
- Principle 5 – Let the other person save face.
- Principle 6 – Praise the slightest improvement and praise every improvement. Be hearty in your approbation and lavish in your praise.

---

[1] Kang, Peter. 2021. "Visualizing Dale Carnegie's How to Win Friends and Influence People - Peter Kang." Peter Kang. January 24, 2021.
https://www.peterkang.com/visualizing-dale-carnegies-how-to-win-friends-influence-people/.

- Principle 7 – Give the other person a fine reputation to live up to.
- Principle 8 – Use encouragement. Make the fault seem easy to correct.
- Principle 9 – Make the other person happy about doing the thing you suggest."[1]

Nobody wants to do good and not be recognized as a doer of good in the material world, but that is exactly what is expected in the spiritual realm. Well, at least that is what I believe. By resisting the urge to openly fight a battle I could not win, I found that I could lead in subtle yet impactful ways — setting an example through my own conduct, quietly advising my subordinates, and still achieving results even with obstacles placed in my path. Though it went against my pride and desire for open vindication, this method of invisible leadership enabled me to stay true to my troop while fulfilling my deeper duty as an officer. I still struggled with whether I was compromising too much, but at the end of the day, I trust that my selfless guidance served as an example and lit the way for others to shine. But I do know this: operating in the shadows allowed me to lead in ways visible leadership could not.

---

**Ansar Saalih, EdD Candidate**
Ansar Saalih is a former Communication & Information Officer in the United States Air Force and leverages four years as an assistant principal at Camden County Technical Schools-GTC and 13 years in the Willingboro, NJ Public School District. He is currently completing his doctoral studies at Wilmington University focused on Organizational Leadership and Innovation.

---

[1] Carnegie, Dale. How to Win Friends and Influence People. New York: Pocket Books, 1936.

# 15

# EQUITY IN MEDICINE
## Surgically Removing the Shame

### AUDREY C. DURRANT, MD

When I came to the US from Canada to attend medical school, I planned to be a Pediatric Neurosurgeon. I had read *Healing Hands* by Dr. Ben Carson. At that time, he was known for being a member of the 1987 surgical team that had separated conjoined twins who were joined at the head. I had no doctors in my family, so this was as close as I had gotten to a surgeon of color.

That was the plan until my 3rd year of medical school during clinical rotations when I had the opportunity to spend quality time with neurosurgeons. It was a disappointment; these were not my people. I didn't enjoy the procedures or the outcomes. I was at a loss; then, I was offered the chance to do an external rotation at Rainbow Babies and Children's with the General Surgeons. It was like a light shining — these were my people.

The problem is my people didn't want me; at the time of my graduation from medical school, no Black female pediatric surgeons were practicing in Canada or the US. The entry door was tightly regulated; at the time, there were only 35 pediatric surgery fellowships in the US and Canada combined, and you were only getting in with an invitation from those already in the field.

My road began at SUNY Downstate, where I found the golden ticket, a mentor, but I still had to do the work and earn one of those 35 fellowship spots.

Surgery is a male-dominated field, so much so that in my intern year, we had an attending who never bothered to learn your name; he just called you "the boy" regardless of your assigned gender because most surgeons were male, so he was correct most of the time.

I was not the first black female pediatric surgeon; that honor belongs to Dr. Andrea Hayes-Jordan, who in 2002, became the first to be board certified in pediatric surgery after being rejected three times. She got her chance at the University of Toronto. So, I followed her footsteps and chose the University of Toronto for my pediatric surgery research fellowship.

In my final year of surgical residency in 2008, Joelle Pierre and I, both women of color, matched in Pediatric Surgery fellowships. That alone was an accomplishment.

I came from a legacy of greatness as SUNY Downstate had a history of training many great surgeons of color, when I went to Oregon Health & Science University Hospital (OHSU) to start my pediatric surgery fellowship, I was confident and strong, like a big dog.

I watched an Instagram reel in which the speaker recounts that she has a big dog, 60-70 pounds, that she lovingly named Cocoa. When Cocoa was a puppy, she would stand Cocoa in front of the mirror, and Cocoa would lick the mirror. Fast forward a few years later, her son put the mirror in front of Cocoa, and she ran. Cocoa had forgotten she was a big dog, and now her reflection scared her. The moral was not to forget that you are a big dog. In medicine, people have often tried to make me forget that I am a big dog.

I was matched at OHSU in Portland, Oregon, for my fellowship. There are at least four applicants for each of the 35 fellowship spots, so you can understand it was a dogfight to get a spot. At graduation, I should have been the program's 4<sup>th</sup> fellow. I was their 3<sup>rd</sup> as I arrived; I found that my initial senior fellow, an Asian woman (the first female accepted to the program), quit in her senior year...to give up when so close to the finish line was unimaginable.

I soon came to understand why. The program was structured, so you spent one year at the main hospital with Dr. Mark Silen, the program director. Then, you spent your senior year in the community hospital, Emmanuel, under the direction of Dr. David W. Bliss.

There were five Attendants, and one thing was easy to read: these men did not like each other, but more importantly, they did not like women surgeons.

My hoped-for mentor, Dr. Silen, was unapproachable and sometimes outright hostile. Why they chose me from the match, I will never understand.

During an overnight call, one of the attendants took me aside to tell me Dr. Silen did not like me. This incident occurred close to the end of my junior year. The intern warned that I needed to shape up if I wanted to succeed during the next stage of my fellowship when I would be working with him at Emmanuel.

Dr. Silen had given me a favorable initial performance evaluation. After this exchange, I was concerned that Dr. Silen would not advance me, but I sailed through without reservations.

As there were two main attendings at Emmanuel, I hoped that if Dr. Bliss' partner was not actively hostile towards me, I could survive, if not thrive. His partner told me that things would go better with Dr. Bliss. This statement made me very uncomfortable as the overtones implied a "tit for tat" that, for a woman who some consider physically attractive made me very nervous. If I reported this concern, it would seem like I thought too highly of my physical attributes.

In addition, Dr. W. Bliss was significantly shorter than me, at 5 ft 9. When you added operating room (OR) clogs, my "working height" was closer to 5 ft 10. He would never raise the OR table when we operated together, requiring me to lean over for hours.

Having to bend over may seem petty, but he could easily make himself taller by standing on a step stool. I could not become shorter, and the physical strain on my back was significant.

Cases I had done and taught as a chief resident in general Surgery were now outside of my abilities. This declaration did not make sense because if not for choosing to continue training in Pediatric Surgery, then and now, I am a fully trained adult general surgeon and would have had attending privileges.

These attendings told me that they had received complaints from the hospital staff about me, and when I asked for details (in hopes of addressing any concerns), neither gave specifics, and one stated, "he was not going to play that game." "They attacked me personally, stating I was rude. My education stalled, and now I was afraid to ask basic questions for fear of being perceived as challenging their authority. On more than one occasion, an attending waved his finger in my face like I was an errant dog; it was humiliating.

This was very different from the treatment my junior resident received, a white male who was also in the Army (I still don't know why the Army needs a pediatric surgeon). They "thanked him for his service" repeatedly, so I wondered if we were at war.

Even how I held my body was criticized as standing with my hand on my hip was perceived as arrogant and a sign of disrespect, and I was called "uppity." We all know what that dog whistle means.

Life at the hospital was taking a significant toll on my emotional and physical well-being. I stopped eating, and I ran more (it is my stress reliever), and as a result, I lost a significant amount of weight, to the point where those who did care about me began to remark on how thin I was becoming.

I made the mistake of confiding in two co-workers that the environment at Emmanuel was untenable. These co-workers then shared my comments with Dr. Silen, who called a meeting with me to discuss the situation. He acknowledged that he was aware that several residents and staff had expressed dissatisfaction with Dr.

Bliss and encouraged me to make a formal complaint to the Director of Graduate Medical Education (GME). I was afraid that this would make things far worse, but he assured me that I had his protection from retaliation. Dr. Silen even accompanied me to meet with the Director to file a formal complaint. I now realize that he had his agenda for Dr. Bliss at OHSU, and he was using me; I was a means to an end.

And as you can imagine, this made everything worse.

Medicine is a team sport, and I got benched.

Whatever little teaching I received by observing Dr. Bliss stopped. What was low level was now palpable.

What Dr. Bliss could not do, his partner could; he increased his aggressive behavior to show his alliance. I was accused of lying on rounds when I stated that my potassium level was 4 when it was 3.8 (there is no clinical significance between potassium of 4 and 3.8).

I met with Dr. Silen for my 6-month evaluation as a senior. As I had a good review, I broached the subject of being moved from Emmanuel. I was not getting an education, and the residents could feel the hostility, and they, too, wisely walked on eggshells. But as we know, the "fish rots from the head down," and nothing changed.

My boyfriend was applying to law school then and said I had no choice but to escalate. So, to protect my interests, I filed a complaint with the OHSU Affirmative Action and Equal Opportunity (AAEO) office, stating that Emmanuel was a hostile work environment.

Within a week of filing my complaint and meeting with an OHSU rep, the team Bliss Attending kicked me under the OR table; during the AAEO investigation, he confirmed that he did kick me but only did that to get me to move and only used a small amount of force.

To this day, he has never offered an apology.

Shortly after this, I met with Dr. Silen; I was sure he would outline how we would restructure the program to move me from Emmanuel. Instead, I was shocked to learn that he was no longer sure that I would graduate from the fellowship and that I should not bother looking for a job for the upcoming year, which, of course, in seeing the light at the end of the tunnel, I had begun a job search. This declaration was a surprise as my evaluations had been good and shown appropriate progression to date. I was in good academic standing, not subject to any disciplinary action, and my test scores had been consistent with the national average. He could not give examples of behaviors that needed to be corrected, and he did not have a remediation plan.

Again, I moved up the chain and made an appointment to speak with the Dean of the Medical School. I don't know what I was expecting. Still, instead of listening to my concerns with empathy, I was chastised for having spoken with the GME first instead of Dr. John Hunter, Dr. Silen's direct supervisor, even though I had followed Dr. Silen's direction. I got another meeting with the GME in which he promised to speak with Dr. Silen about personally mentoring me, and he assured me that I would graduate as he saw nothing from my program reviews that would indicate otherwise.

During this time, Dr. Bliss abruptly departed from OHSU. Dr. Silen left the main hospital to direct Emmanuel until a replacement was found or announced.

I optimistically also began interviewing for Pediatric Surgery, attending jobs at the University of Chicago, UCLA Children's, and Children's Hospital of New Orleans. I had friends in all three cities, and my applications were enthusiastically met. I would have been happy at any of these locations. But when I got back, I was ghosted. I contacted my mentors and contacts to find out what had happened. They told me that when these hospitals had reached out to OHSU for a reference, I was being blackballed by my program.

I felt so betrayed. And then the final shoe dropped. Dr. Silen gave me my final 6-month evaluation. This one was so different from my others, it seemed to be about a different person. I would not be graduating as a pediatric surgeon at the end of the year, and there was no plan for remediation. As per Dr. Silen, I need an additional year of training for him to consider signing off on my graduation. As there were only 35 programs in the country and to graduate, each fellow needed a specific number of index cases (classic examples of unique instances to pediatric surgery practice – i.e., malrotation or tracheoesophageal fistulas), no program had a sufficiently large enough volume of teaching cases to be able to take an additional fellow beyond those in the matching process. He was killing my dream.

Dr. Silen suggested he would be willing to investigate the possibility of me training elsewhere, but only if I showed him, "I was worth it."

I contacted the fellow who quit and found out she had received the same treatment. I asked why she didn't report the harassment, and she said she had spoken with Dr. Silen, but it had gone no further; she didn't want to be "that girl." So she quit; and because she was a good surgeon, was able to get a spot in a Plastic Surgery Fellowship.

It almost broke me. But my boyfriend was mad; he saw his once self-assured and competent partner now not even able to order dinner at a restaurant without fear.

We found a fantastic employment attorney, Dana Sullivan (I still count her as a friend today). And she spoke in the only words that matter to the hospital: money and litigation.

Being kicked was assault, and she made sure that I documented everything (which I had; I have had a diary since I was 16). We contacted Downstate, who still had accreditation for a pediatric surgery program, and I went home.

It took an additional year, but I became a pediatric surgeon, and OHSU fired Dr. Silen (who no longer practices medicine, as my report empowered other OHSU residents to disclose years of harassment and misogyny).

I didn't get to walk at graduation and had no one to support my job search, but there was no one to tank it.

And I wish I could end with, "and she lived happily ever after."

But we know it does not, as I felt shame for what occurred at OHSU — shame that I let these men almost break me; shame that I did not have a program supporting me during my job search.

Shame says, "I am bad," and guilt says that the "behavior is bad." And when we stay focused on shame, it can sometimes become associated with a lack of self-care, depression, and suicide.

We need to let go of shame. We, as physicians of color, have been led to believe that we should be grateful to be in the spaces we occupy, like it was a gift and not the result of our innate talents and hard work. But I know differently.

So, out of my trials emerged purpose. I started a movement called White Coat Green Room to promote diversity and inclusion in medicine. Just as Victor Green's Negro Motorist Green Book guided African Americans to safe passage in the 1930s, the White Coat Green Room provides a space for physicians of color to come together. Here, we can have the difficult but necessary conversations, share our stories, advocate for change, and support one another.

There is joy to be found in healing, and the Green Room helps sustain that. My trials have given me insight and purpose — I now work to light the way for those who come after me.

---

**Dr. Audrey C. Durrant**

www.whitecoatgreenroom.com

Dr. Audrey C. Durrant is a dedicated clinical assistant professor and pediatric surgeon committed to teaching, innovation, and providing exceptional minimally invasive care to underserved children. Her passion lies in pushing medicine forward as an ally while addressing systemic issues, merging scientific advancement with compassion.

# NAVIGATING WORKPLACE BIASES AND POLITICS

1.  How have you navigated workplace dynamics that challenge
    your identity, and what strategies have helped you advocate
    for yourself?

    _____

    _____

    _____

    _____

    _____

    _____

    _____

    _____

    _____

    _____

    _____

    _____

    _____

    _____

    _____

    _____

    _____

    _____

    _____

    _____

    _____

    _____

    _____

    _____

    _____

2. How have workplace biases—whether implicit or explicit—impacted your career growth, and what strategies can you use to challenge or navigate them effectively?

_____

_____

_____

_____

_____

_____

_____

_____

_____

_____

_____

_____

_____

_____

_____

_____

_____

_____

_____

_____

_____

_____

_____

_____

_____

# MAINTAINING MENTAL WELLNESS AT WORK

1. What steps can you take to protect your mental health while maintaining authenticity in spaces that may not fully embrace you?

_____

_____

_____

_____

_____

_____

_____

_____

_____

_____

_____

_____

_____

_____

_____

_____

_____

_____

_____

_____

2. How does your work environment impact your emotional well-being, and what boundaries can you set to foster balance and resilience?

_____

_____

_____

_____

_____

_____

_____

_____

_____

_____

_____

_____

_____

_____

_____

_____

_____

_____

_____

_____

_____

_____

_____

_____

# CREATING FINANCIAL FREEDOM BEYOND THE 9-TO-5

1. What financial strategies can you implement today to create long-term security and reduce reliance on traditional employment?

_____
_____
_____
_____
_____
_____
_____
_____
_____
_____
_____
_____
_____
_____
_____
_____
_____
_____
_____
_____
_____
_____

2. How can collective economic empowerment within your community help shift generational wealth and financial stability?

# CONTINUE THE TRIUMPH SERIES

If this book inspired you, don't stop here.

Explore the next volumes with new stories and insights at: www.theauthorsjourney.co/triumph

www.ingramcontent.com/pod-product-compliance
Lightning Source LLC
Chambersburg PA
CBHW060420130626
46555CB00005B/2140